GUIDES

Mystical Connections to Soul Guides and Divine Teachers

Enjoy these other books in the Common Sentience series:

ANCESTORS: *Divine Remembrances of Lineage, Relations and Sacred Sites*

ANGELS: *Personal Encounters with Divine Beings of Light*

ANIMALS: *Personal Tales of Encounters with Spirit Animals*

ASCENSION: *Divine Stories of Awakening the Whole and Holy Being Within*

MEDITATION: *Intimate Experiences with the Divine through Contemplative Practices*

NATURE: *Divine Experiences with Trees, Plants, Stones and Landscapes*

SHAMANISM: *Personal Quests of Communion with Nature and Creation*

SOUND: *Profound Experiences with Chanting, Toning, Music and Healing Frequencies*

Learn more at sacredstories.com.

GUIDES

Mystical Connections to Soul Guides and Divine Teachers

Featuring

MARILYN ALAURIA

Sacred Stories
PUBLISHING

Books may be purchased through booksellers or by contacting Sacred Stories Publishing.

Guides: Mystical Connections to Soul Guides and Divine Teachers
Marilyn Alauria

Print ISBN: 978-1-945026-97-3
EBook ISBN: 978-1-945026-98-0

Library of Congress Control Number: 2022935257

Published by Sacred Stories Publishing, Fort Lauderdale, FL USA

CONTENTS

PART THREE: DEEPENING YOUR CONNECTION WITH YOUR GUIDES

APPENDIX: PICK YOUR GUIDE
MEET OUR SACRED STORYTELLERS
MEET OUR FEATURED AUTHOR

PART ONE

Understanding Guides

Your heart knows the way.
Run in that direction.

—RUMI

JOURNEY WITH YOUR GUIDES

◆

*A*re you ready to go on a journey with your guides to co-create your most infinite and magical experience? They are inviting you. All you have to do is say yes, and you will be on your way.

Try it! Close your eyes, say "Yes!" out loud to see how it feels, and then breathe.

This book is an invitation to live every single day of your life in connection with your guides. Before I consciously knew what guides are or that we all have them, my soul experienced deep conversations with these beings through dreams, prayers, and feelings that something greater than us exists and is here to support us. During the most crucial moments in my life—with my outstretched desires reaching into the darkness—I would wonder, *Am I alone? Am I safe?*

I couldn't articulate the rumblings in my heart, but at moments, my inner awareness caught glimpses of a faint, shimmering light guiding me to its love. Before I finally met my guides, a love affair with something greater than me had danced in and out of my life.

Then, the moment happened. I found them, and we have been dancing through life together every day since.

Our guides invite us into a conversation with them. They help guide us to our highest truth and wisdom and help us discover a deeper understanding and experience. They never take our power away; they empower us, bringing us to our own truth, which is more amazing than we can imagine.

There is no right or wrong way to work with your guides. With some great tools and techniques, which I will describe in this book, you will learn your instrument, the way you communicate with your guides, and how to follow their directions.

The important first step: You have to invite them. That is how you start. Many times, people wait for their guides to show up, but by waiting, guess what happens? You don't see them. It's not that they aren't there; you aren't participating in the conversation.

Before I met my guides, my life was a bit of a mess. I was pursuing avenues that I thought were the desires of my soul. Yet I was miserable, depressed, and felt alone, struggling to understand what I needed to do to change my life. After I met my guides, my life made more sense.

About seven years ago, I was going through an especially difficult time, and my guides kept saying, *Lean into us; lean into us.* I would lean into them and feel their safety. In my most anxious moments, a sense of peace would wash over me, and I knew, without any doubt, that I am unconditionally loved by my guides all of the time.

Our guides' main reason for working with us is to help us live from our souls. They want us to tap into our wisdom and live a spiritual life in human form—a life filled with guidance and unconditional love—and to fulfill our mission, the reason we are here. Our guides can help us discover how to be fully in love with ourselves—and that kind of love helps us to have incredible lives. Don't you agree?

Why do our guides care so much about the details of our lives? Because in our souls—in the deepest part of our beings—*we* care so much. Our guides reflect our highest truths, our souls, and the loving universe we live in. When

I asked mine why they cared, they responded, *Because you care, that's why we care.*

Once I understood that, and knew I wasn't alone, my soul felt like: *Okay, I can do this life because you're here with me, and you're going to do it with me.*

Maybe right now, you are breathing again because you got a piece of your own puzzle through hearing my story. Take another deep breath, and let's continue this journey together.

Invite your guides to help you understand your own reason for being here. Breathe into that question and trust that the answer will come as you develop a relationship with your guides.

Maybe you already know your guides and are looking to meet a new one or to deepen your connection. Or this might be your first foray into meeting them. No matter where you are, I invite you to go on a deeper journey with your guides by taking them along with you as you read. Ask them to be by your side right now and point out the moments in this book that are meant to carry you to your dreams and desires.

Your guides will give you whatever help you ask for. They are here to help you navigate the journey of your life. They brought you to this book for a reason. Trust that through reading this book with them, you will gain access to the secrets within your soul. All you need is intention and trust in the process. Make a declaration now. Say it out loud:

"My intention is to take this journey with you. I know you are here with me. I promise to trust you as we read this book together."

How did that feel? That's all it takes. People complicate their relationships with their guides. It's so much simpler than you can imagine. In these pages, I will show you just how easy it can be. Your guides want you to live the life you desire, to remove the brackets of limitations from your dreams. They want you to trust the urges you have in your heart and follow them. They might not take you where you set out to go, but they will take you to where you are meant to be, and you'll find it more extraordinary than you can imagine. Your destiny is so much better than you think.

How do I know? Because my guides have done this for me, countless times. They have been with me every step of the way. From the day I met my first guide until the moment I began authoring this book, my life has changed into a delightful co-creation that continues to surprise me. Each day, I wake up excited to live my life, knowing I'm supported, loved, and always shown the way.

The time is now to step out in faith, trust, and surrender to this exciting journey with your guides. Your new life is about to begin. Enjoy.

A RELATIONSHIP WITH YOUR GUIDES

---◆---

*I*magine entering into a relationship with someone you have never met who is loving, supportive, and caring—someone who sees you, hears you, and has your best interests at heart. This connection transcends time and is one of the most supportive loves you will ever know. Can you let go of expectation and open your heart to that experience? This is the connection you can have with your guides.

We come to this Earth plane with one or more guides, depending on our soul plan. Our guides have been with us since before birth; some have accompanied us in other incarnations, as well. We knew about them before we were born, and they've known about us.

Our connection with our guides is a relationship. On Earth, we learn everything through relationships. Think about it. You have a relationship with your parents, siblings, friends, teachers, nature, animals, and yourself. It's no different with your guides. Just as you're in a relationship with your family and friends, you are in a relationship with your guides. And when you meet your guides, you must work on the relationship, as you must with any relationship in your life. You're getting to know and trust them and growing in intimacy. And they are doing the same with you. They are learning how you work, how you listen, how you learn, and how you grow, because they need that information to guide you to your greatest potential.

Your relationship is personal and specific to you. It's your footprint. For example, I have three siblings. During a traumatic event, we were all different ages. We have different memories and different experiences of that same event, and because of that, each of us has a different relationship with the family now. It's the same with our guides.

Your relationship with your guides is specific to you and your life experiences. For example, you and I both might have Archangel Michael as a guide. He will communicate with you using your life experiences, the symbolic language of your soul, how you learn, how you feel, and all your other unique qualities. Therefore, we could both be talking with him and have the same question, but we would receive completely different information. His relationship with you is unique to the two of you, just as your relationship with your mother is different than anyone else's. No two people share the same experiences in life. Even if we had the same parents, we had different teachers, loves, interests, and books we read. Therefore, your relationship with your guides is as unique as you are.

You also can have a deeper bond with certain guides because you've traveled different lifetimes with them, or they've been your guide before. It's important to deepen into and understand the intricacies and intimacies of the level of relationships you can have with your guides. Your guides are fully accepting and loving. That is the true feeling of your relationship with them. They don't judge—ever. I have never had an experience in which I said, "I've done this, and I did this and this," and they met my words with anything but an incredible amount of love, understanding, and guidance. They truly embody the meaning of unconditional love.

Does that mean they always agree with our actions? Not necessarily, but they don't disagree, either. They use some events as teachable moments that help us grow. Their love and support also help us grow. They meet us where we are and offer so much love, despite any shame we might be experiencing because of the choices we've made. They don't hold onto any of that; they completely accept us. Then, they direct us to learn why something may have happened the way it did, how to heal, and how to make our next choices and move forward. They help us understand what character traits the experience might have instilled in us to prepare us for something yet to come. They are helping us to become the best humans we can be in this incarnation. They know our dreams and desires, and they want us to develop the traits we need to meet our experiences with confidence and joy.

WHEN GUIDES SHOW UP

Many times, we feel urgings inside of us telling us there's something bigger—something greater—for us. Our guides appear when we are ready to own our existence. They arrive to find us struggling with something and willing to take a different path or make a better choice. When we are ready to be seen, and to stand in our mission and live the life we are meant to live, our guides show us how we can accomplish this. Their goal is to help us live the life we envision—the one in our hearts.

Guides are always there. We might not see them if we're not ready to do so, or if we're not open to seeing them because we're stuck in a problem. If we don't feel worthy of their love, we might shut our hearts down to them.

But when we open our hearts and say, "I know I'm meant for something more. Please guide me," it's like a film across our eyes disappears, and our consciousness comes into view. The way we perceive the world starts dissolving or vanishes, and our guides become apparent.

When we get into the place of really wanting to communicate with them, the intention of wanting is enough, and they will show up. And when they do, every experience in the universe becomes a magical dance.

Our guides also can be teachers that step in momentarily. When I was opening to my mediumship skill, three guides came in. They were with me for a brief time to teach me a certain part of mediumship, and they let me know that. If you have a particular skill you want to learn, you can call on a guide who is an expert in that field to help you. You can call on one you know of—like Einstein or Picasso—or ask Spirit to send you the most appropriate guide. When you call on a particular guide (like Einstein or Picasso), ask if you have their soul's permission to help you. If you get a no, choose someone else. There are plenty of experts to help you get to where you want to go.

Here's another fun fact: You even can call on the energy of a living person who is an expert in a particular field to help. Knowledge is energy. It travels and is available to you. For example, say you want to work with the energy of a teacher you admire. Ask to connect with their energy and feel it next to you. In this case, you don't have to ask for the soul's permission, because you are asking for the energy to support you. If you feel attraction to this person, it's because what they have is also inside of you, and you need only ask the universe and your guides to light it up.

HOW LONG OUR GUIDES STAY

We all have at least one guide that stays with us from birth until we transition. Other guides will appear at different points in our lives or interact with each other, depending on what we need at the time. They may evolve past what they're teaching us and move on to something else—or we might evolve past our need for them.

Once we develop relationships with our guides, we may be unable to imagine living without them. But that is our consciousness today, based on where we are in our life experience. Our guides shift as we shift, and when our consciousness elevates, certain guides will leave because we no longer need their assistance. We have already reached the consciousness they were here to assist us with, so their work is complete. Another guide with another expertise will come in to support us.

When it is time for a guide to leave, they don't just vanish, because when we get to know someone, we love them, and they love us. If they were to go away tomorrow, that might leave a huge hole in our heart. Our guides understand this part of the relationship, so when they're getting ready to go, they help us become accustomed to the energy of their going away. It's a process that is quite magical and beautiful.

However, if we entered the relationship with our guides feeling that they were not going to be with us forever; that might affect our connection and our ability to relate to them, based on our level of safety and security. It's important to experience your guides while they're with you and know that they'll be there as long as you need them; and when you no longer need them, you will be ready for them to go.

You can see how much our guides care because they don't just abandon us when their task is done. They give us the opportunity to say goodbye. I can always tell when a guide is about to leave because they start to fade, but I don't feel sad or that I'm going to miss them. I know that our time together is ending, and we are departing on beautiful terms. The experience gives new meaning to the word "closure." Our farewell is a tying-up of loose ends and a respect for their journey as well as my own.

The best I can liken it to is a graduation from school. Your education is complete, and you are saying goodbye, but you're not overwhelmed with sadness, because you feel you no longer need that school's lessons. Instead, at graduation, you feel proud and know you are ready to embark on your next adventure.

Now, let's dive deeper into who our guides are and what they can do.

MEET YOUR GUIDES

---◆---

Our guides have purposes that are big, limitless, infinite, and constantly growing. They know what our soul is here to do and have wisdom that we don't have access to yet. Guides help us access the wisdom within ourselves—to grow, learn, open up to possibilities, and live in alignment with and reflect the truth of our souls.

Our guides co-create and communicate with us through vibration, repetitive signs, sounds, and energy. They help us interpret the meaning of symbols and synchronicities in our dance with the universe. If the universe is bringing you a message, your guides' role is to help you interpret it. They know what your soul needs: to live your highest, most expansive experience— to live the dreams that are in your heart. Those dreams are to be enjoyed, not forgotten.

Sometimes, the dreams for our lives don't show up the way we visualize them because we imagine them from a limited mindset, because of our past experiences. Whenever we put wisdom or life experience into a container, we lose the essence of why we're really here. We also lose the extent of what a guide can do.

Guides vary in their expertise. Some assist us in daily life or in the evolution of our consciousness on our longer journey. They can help us develop skills and a deeper understanding; protect us and help us feel safe; and show us love in new ways. Guides are our support system for living the highest experience of our soul. With their guidance, we learn how to take the reins of our lives, make powerful decisions, and live!

Our guides reflect what we need to learn at that moment, where we need to grow, and how we need to understand our journey in this world. They ask us to believe in the magic that's greater than we can see. They help us own the dreams in our hearts and take action to make them happen. Then, they ask us to surrender our dreams to something greater. They guide us on our path as we make choices toward that dream—and when it comes to fruition, it's more incredible than we thought.

Their invitation is to develop a relationship with them that is outside the parameters of what we already know. Our guides want us to think limitlessly because they offer us a multitude of consciousness. If a guide shows up to us as one form, it could be one, three, or a thousand different types of energies coming together into one consciousness.

Guides work with our understanding, and while they want us to be limitless in what we know and to grow in our awareness, they also work with our levels of consciousness. As our consciousness increases and expands, they can work with us more. As we grow, they grow. They meet us where we are, teaching us about the endless possibilities and magic in this life. For example, they once told me I was dreaming with brackets on.

"Are you crazy? I'm dreaming so big!" I said.

No, you are dreaming with limitation based on your past experience. You aren't dreaming from what is available to you because you don't know what you can truly have. Take the brackets off your dreams and believe that what can show up is so much greater than you can imagine, they replied.

I constantly live by their suggestion—to take the brackets off and surrender—and what shows up continues to amaze me.

ROLES GUIDES PLAY

Guides can play distinct roles in our lives. For example, you can have a Love Guide, Health Guide, and an Overall Guide. The bottom line is, you have a guide, whether you pick one or they pick you. It's the same thing. Let me explain. People often tell me that they are struggling to meet their guide. When I question them further, I realize they are waiting for the skies to open and their guide to materialize in front of them. When I probe a little more, I usually find out they are already talking to their guide, but they haven't given it credibility. They are usually in conversation with Archangel Michael, Jesus, or a grandparent—yet they weren't thinking this was their guide. Why not? They didn't think it could be that easy. And when we talk further, they realize that it is. So, don't wait for the clouds to part to reveal your guide. Pick one now.

Who do you feel safe with, love, and have an affinity for? Archangel Michael? Jesus? Someone else? Pick one you feel safe with and trust they are your guide for now. Work with them for a few weeks, and you will learn how to communicate. People complicate it—get into their heads—but it's easier than you think.

Let's go through some of the types of guides, so you have a better understanding of the roles they can play. I refer to guides as she and he in these examples because I learned relationship through masculine and feminine roles. As we know, these roles have grown and expanded. How you relate to gender might determine how your guides may choose to show up. In other words, there are no fixed rules about how you experience your guides. The beauty of this work with them is that it is always expanding. The information is infinite. Let it flow.

GATEKEEPER GUIDE

The Gatekeeper Guide is the one who can connect you to all your other guides. He or she serves as a protector of sorts, standing by your side as you're working with different guides, and is the one that allows them in or doesn't allow them in. Your gatekeeper guide also can be a bridge for you, because you must raise your vibration to meet your guides, and they must lower their vibration to meet you.

Before you can raise your vibration easily, you can ask your gatekeeper guide to help you. My gatekeeper guide would do that for me. He would help me raise my vibration to communicate with my guides, and he would help make the connection fast and direct. He'd help me know which guide was the right one for me and then serve as a layer of protection so that not just anyone could come in.

My gatekeeper guide is a male energy, and he's interesting because he'll just walk the perimeter. When I first started opening to my guides, my gatekeeper was the first guide who appeared to me. He taught me that when a guide appears, you have to ask the guide, "Are you from my highest light and in highest alignment with me?"

It's my experience that they answer honestly. They'll say either yes or no. If they say no, you ask them to leave, and you go to the next guide that comes in. You have free will; if you don't like what comes in, tell it to go.

MAIN GUIDE

Main Guides can act as the leader of the group, but they don't tell the other guides what to do. They are holding the energy for all the other guides and you. They have been with you for a long time. You two decided to come into this life together, although they don't like to reveal too much of who they are to you. They want you to develop your relationship with them over time.

Main Guides are strong, like loyal best friends who always have your back and love you no matter what you do. But with that love, they are there to guide you and tell you the truth. They help you stay the course, be true to yourself, and honor your dreams and desires. They help you to not lie to yourself and to see the way of your heart. They are the light of your path. Like lighthouses, they shine all around you and especially in front of you.

Your relationship with your main guide transcends time. My main guide wants me to tell you: *That is all you need to know because this is a relationship that is so special to you that words in a book could never do it the justice it deserves.*

TEACHING GUIDE

Teaching Guides come in when you need to become an expert or feel like an expert in some field. Think of it as taking a class in a particular subject. That teacher has studied in that area, and they are going to teach you what they know for the time you are in that class. They don't stay with you for long, but they help you develop skills and learn things you desire to learn.

You can call upon an expert in an area; you can even call upon an expert you know. If you are studying art, you can ask for a guide to come in and teach you about watercolors, or you can ask for a specific artist known for watercolor art. The only caveat is that not every artist is available to work with you. So, if you call someone in, and you don't feel their presence around you, try someone else.

How do you call them in? Just set an intention of what you want to learn. Then ask and trust they will show up. Asking aloud is super helpful. You can even write down your request and read it out loud. Intention is everything in this work. When you set an intention and believe it can happen, it does.

GUIDES FOR SPECIFIC ROLES

Since guides are here to help us live our most infinite experiences, we can have several types of guides to support us. If you're desiring to explore and learn in a key area of your life, you can request guides with specific expertise to come in to support you, creating your own loving and energetic support team. When I was doing readings, I wanted guides in specific areas like health and love, so I called them in. They are still with me while I write this book and they probably will be with me for a long time. I also called in a marketing guide to work with me. It was different than a teaching guide because I knew I wanted one for a long time.

Teaching guides will usually be there for a brief period of time and will come in and out. When you ask for a guide in a certain area to be a part of your team, they are with you for a long time.

To do this in a meditation, you could say, "I want to meet my health guide. Can my health guide come in?" I will take you through the process of meeting a guide later in the book.

A **Health Guide** can tell you which doctor to go to, what foods to eat, or what protocols are good for you.

A **Business Guide** can give you tips that you can use in your business—things you may not have thought about.

For love in all relationships, a **Love Guide** is amazing. They encompass more than romantic relationships; they help with family and friends or feeling love for animals and our planet.

Philosophy Guides help you form belief systems to live by. They are quite knowledgeable and fun. They will share what happens when we leave this planet, what to believe in, and what to let go of. They really are an endless source of information. Pull up a chair and start talking to these guides, and you will learn things that will blow you away.

A **Joy Guide** can help you have fun and get in touch with your playful side.

Guides can help us in many ways. The ones above are the ones I have had experience with, but this work is always growing, so the list is growing. What kind of guide would you like to have?

POSITIONING YOUR GUIDES AND WHY IT'S IMPORTANT

While our guides want us to think limitlessly, they understand the parameters that give us structure and a sense of security. Because we learn through relationship and they want to support us, we can put our guides in various places around us to better communicate with them.

Think about it. When you are walking and talking with a friend, they may be walking to the right of you, so your attention is on them. Knowing where your guide stands—and they stand in that same place all the time—helps you develop a relationship with them. You expect them to be there, they are there, and now you can easily communicate with them.

When you meet your guides, tell them where to stand and ask them to stand there all the time. This also helps as you move about your day. It doesn't matter where you go; they go with you and are always in the same place, even when you aren't. For example, your health guide could be to your right and your love guide to your left, and whenever you need to communicate with them, they are in that place, even if you are hiking on a trail or sitting in your meditation space. And like a good friend, when you need them, you can turn to them and start communicating.

Guides also keep a certain proximity to you based on your comfort level. Your health guide may be twenty feet away, but another guide might be two inches away. Some people feel their guides in their hearts, and they never move from there. Whether your guides are inside your physical being or outside your physical being, they are always where you expect them to be. Your inner awareness is on them, and they are answering you.

There is another reason positioning your guide is important: It helps you focus on your guide despite all the distractions that may be trying to get your attention. If you are talking to your guide and know they are on the right side of you, your inner awareness is fixed on them. Let's try it now.

Pick a place you would like your guide to stand and bring your awareness to them. Focus on them in that location. If you close your eyes and direct your attention to them, your inner awareness is on them once again. Now breathe with them. Send them breath and they are sending you breath. You are now creating a line of energy consisting of breath that connects you two. The more you work with this, the more powerful it becomes, and your relationship gets so strong that outside disruptions never invade your connection with your guides.

GENDER AND WHAT FEELS SAFE

Your guides can be female, male, or androgynous beings. The identification with gender is for us. Most people have a strong understanding of what feminine and masculine energies feel like, and our guides use gender to help us understand the qualities they possess. Their energies will typically match the energies we associate with the gender, because it feels safe for us.

My gatekeeper guide is very tall and large and has a masculine energy because that's what feels safe to me in his role. But someone else may find that a masculine energy doesn't feel safe to them, so their gatekeeper won't be masculine. That's why our physical beings are the instruments our guides work through. They know what we relate to. They determine who we might be open to, and they embody that energy.

When someone says, "I met my guide, and I'm scared," it's usually because the guide came in with unconditional love, and they experience it as fear. Initially, they can't receive their guide in the purest form. But once they tune in more, they can feel and receive the love.

In life, there are synchronicities and perceived good and bad moments. When we feel like we've gotten knocked off course or we get a "no" from something, we may think, "Oh, I'm not . . ."

Many times, we may think the universe is responding to something we did wrong or that we didn't do enough. In reality, you may be holding onto something that isn't aligned with you. Or it might be that your guides are saving you from going down a road that might not have been good for you. That "no" moment might be a character-building experience, and you're learning something about yourself, so you can meet the "yes" moment when it arrives.

Everything is information. Your guides are filling in and filtering what you need to know. They are your teachers, wise friends, and biggest cheerleaders, enticing you to try something new. Who wouldn't want to walk the Earth plane with them? They make life colorful and fun and help you live aligned with your soul.

TYPES OF GUIDES

———————◆———————

*G*uides communicate using a multidimensional language that transcends time and space. They can incarnate in many ways: as ascended beings, deceased loved ones, angels, animals, nature, planets, color, beings from other dimensions and star systems. We're able to connect with different entities and energies because everything is physical relationship—relationship with them, relationship with our soul, relationship with the universe, and relationship with planets. We are in relationship and co-creation.

Consider what we discussed about relationships. There can be four siblings with the same father and the same mother, and yet a relationship with them will be different for each sibling. It's the same thing with guides; your relationship with the moon will be different than someone else's relationship with the moon. I may not resonate with the sun, whereas other people may have a strong resonance with the sun. It is such an intimate relationship, and it's important to cultivate the relationship based on your own personal feelings or intuitive hits. That's why I keep coming back to the idea that you are the instrument through which you receive information. Learn how to read and use your instrument.

Each entity is a reflection for us. It's our relationship to that entity on this Earth plane—however we understand it—that creates a different co-creation or opportunity for growth for each of us. No one can have the exact relationship you have with your guides, because it's personal to you. Don't try to assign rules or fit your communication with your guides in a box. Instead, unwrap that box, cut the sides, let the sides collapse, and let your relationship with your guides take the shape that serves you. When you approach this relationship from a limitless consciousness, you will be amazed at the guidance you have access to. Let's explore some of the ways our guides can connect with us.

PLANETS AND COSMOS

The planets and cosmos teach us there's something much greater out there. We have a consciousness or understanding that there's a mystery, and we're trying to learn it.

When I walk outside, there is one star that I feel I have a relationship with. I don't know the name of the star, but I know where it is in the sky. I'm drawn to it. So, whenever I'm having a particularly difficult moment or am feeling lost, I'll go out on my deck, and I'll see that star staring at me. I just breathe . . . breathe in energy with that star, and I automatically feel connected to something greater than me, which allows me to release what is restricting me or troubling me. Then, I can open to something bigger—more possibilities, more solutions. The star is showing me that it's guiding me. It's making me feel something, awakening something inside of me, so I don't feel alone.

When we resonate with a star, the moon, or specific planets, it's common to wonder if it's a conscious relationship with them or if they are acting more as guiding forces. It's both. We feel a connection—a specificity with things that speak to us. If I look at the moon, the moon is looking at me. I'm attracted to the moon because the moon is attracted to me. I'm not looking at the constellation of Orion or interested in Orion. And therefore, the moon is choosing and guiding me, and then, I'm choosing the moon and accepting the guidance.

ASCENDED BEINGS

Ascended beings have walked this Earth plane and lived a sacred type of life—a life that we could imitate, leading us to our hearts, souls, and healing. They're representatives of a cleaner, clearer, more peaceful path.

These beings are typically referred to as Ascended Masters, but the word "masters" does not work for them. It's a word we gave them. Guides never look at themselves as higher or lower than anyone else, even if they have wisdom that will awaken us to an incredible way of living.

Living beautiful, sacred, peaceful lives, these beings walk their talk. And because we know who they are—there's a history about them—we can connect to them. Because they lived a human life, we can relate to them. They represent a higher path that we can take or show us how to have a spiritual life in human form.

What's interesting about that is what Jesus shows us. He shows us that a spiritual life isn't necessarily easy. You don't choose an enlightened path, and then life is easy. He shows us that through pain, we can evolve into something incredible.

We have seen ascended beings in this lifetime, too. Mother Teresa and Thich Nhat Hanh are two examples. Ascended beings show us how to live a spiritual life—what it's like to be spirit in human form. They are guiding lights for us.

ANGELS

Angels are very pure, beautiful, loving energy. They are the essence of love—true love—and nothing can penetrate true love.

Color is important to the angels because they haven't necessarily incarnated on the Earth plane, although there are times when they can take physical form and walk among us. If I were to apply a color for angels, it would be pink because pink conveys compassion for self, and the angels have an incredible amount of compassion for us.

There are levels of angels within the angelic realm because we have different levels of understanding. We ascribe levels to the angelic realm, so we know where we are and what we need to tap into at a particular moment. An archangel can summon a greater sense of power or safety for us, whereas the little angel by a child's bed can provide an incredible feeling of safety for them. The levels of angels are how we resonate with them, and we can create a strong relationship with that level of the angelic realm.

Angels are a higher consciousness, and we attribute human forms to them so we can relate better. Our angelic guides can take on various roles: a love angel, a protection angel, a home angel, and a money angel are examples. These relationships come more from us than from them. It is their way of creating a relationship with us, so we can access their wisdom.

HIGHER SELF

Your higher self is an aspect of you—a deep reflection of your soul—at a higher but attainable consciousness. Your higher self already holds the wisdom and information you need; to do something you desire to do. It has already walked the journey you want to embark on; therefore, it knows what choices you should make to achieve your goals. It is a wonderful light for your path.

As your guide, your higher self can answer your questions about where you are today to help you achieve the goals in your heart. For example, say you want to author a book and plan to accomplish that goal in three years. In the present, an aspect of yourself has already achieved it. Your higher self is an author and has the wisdom that it will take for you to get there. Therefore, it can be a valuable guide for you.

What's fascinating is, your higher self can show up in different forms. It could be a younger self that held a type of consciousness and wisdom that you didn't necessarily incorporate into your life. It also can show up as a different sex than you. If you are a feminine person in this physical state, your higher self could be a male. Or various physical aspects of your higher self can represent prior incarnations, including specific facial features, animals, or elements of nature. Your relationship with your higher self is limitless, just like you are.

LOVED ONES WHO WALKED THE EARTH PLANE

Deceased loved ones can be your guides if you allow them to evolve on the other side and then let them help you to evolve. If someone has recently transitioned, it's important to give them enough space and time, because when people pass to the other side, they are doing their work, too.

You cannot bring in a deceased loved one as a guide and continue the same relationship with them you had while they were on the Earth plane. If they are to be your guide, you have to let them walk side by side with you and allow their wisdom to come. You can't hold on to how your mother was on the Earth plane or believe that your father on the other side will be the same person he was on this side. You would be doing a disservice to the guidance they can provide.

Often, it is our consciousness that pulls them in. So, when a father comes in, he will come in the body form you recognize so you will feel comfortable. As a guide, he's there to deliver a message to help you live your life on the Earth plane. He will want you to move forward and live your best life yet.

My father came through during the writing of this book. He hadn't fully come through to me since he passed, three years ago. We had a difficult relationship, so I hadn't been ready to receive him. It was a magical experience, because now I felt ready to receive him in his higher-state form. I knew it was him because all his wonderful qualities—not the difficult ones—were there. I fully connected to his brilliance, humor, intuitiveness, belief in me, and creativity. These traits were fleeting when he was on Earth, but I recognized him immediately when he came through.

If a loved one is a guide for years, they are helping you because you need that feeling that the loved one provided for you. A mother spirit will come in to help one of her children on the Earth plane not feel alone—to feel encouraged and loved. I am curious to see how my father wants to assist me, but we need to build on this new relationship first so I can gain trust in him. A relationship that has history, like the ones we have with our loved ones, can be a tremendous support and may evolve beyond what it was before they passed.

OTHERS WHO WALKED THE EARTH PLANE

Well-known people who have transitioned can also be your guide. You may not have known them personally or followed their work, but their energy has an expertise that is helpful to you.

The actor Sal Mineo has been one of the biggest guides for me because he opened me up to believing even more in my mediumship abilities. He taught me how to trust in what I was able to do. The same with Wayne Dyer. I saw Wayne Dyer speak, but I didn't follow his work. When he passed, there was this sudden connection. I recently had stopped drinking because I decided I wanted to take a break, and I feel he was instrumental in that.

People still walking the Earth plane, like the Dalai Lama or another prominent teacher or leader, can also be guides. They can be guides because their energy exists—an energy that can be helpful to you and you can tune in to. Remember what I said before: Take the way you communicate out of the box, and magic will happen.

ANIMALS

Animals act as messengers, teaching us that we have inside of us whatever we need. They bring attention to a specific character trait to adopt or strengthen so that we can move forward in our lives. Their primal instincts represent a strong theme for us, often qualities that we need to open or awaken to, or embody, to make powerful choices and live in stronger alignment with our souls.

Our animal companions are a little different. Since we are in relationship with them, they help us learn more about our own emotions and capabilities. In that way, they can be our greatest teachers, guiding us to our highest truth.

NATURE

Nature gives us a tangible experience of what guides can be. Nature is one way through which our guides can express themselves or connect with us.

The forms our guides take are based on the meaning or symbolism associated with a specific aspect of nature.

This allows us to connect more easily, because people often communicate with guides that they don't necessarily see with their physical eyes. Rather, they may see them with their mind's eye, have a feeling, or sense an energy about them.

Through nature, our guides remind us that there is something bigger than us out there, and they teach us how to tap into the wisdom of our souls. Think about the color of the sky. There are certain moments when you're just taking in the blue, the orange, or the red of a sunset. That's a moment of expansion, an opening, when the colors guide you into higher realms— higher experiences. You can't deny those moments.

TREES

Trees reach up into the sky; they're closer to God, or the universe, and they represent what guidance can be for us and do for us. They're majestic, symbolizing beauty, protection, and support. They also are very grounding. Trees reach down into the ground and reach high up into the sky. They represent the spiritual life on the Earth plane.

Trees show us we can have a physical relationship with nature in an enchanting way. When you have a relationship with a tree, it can be a real, authentic relationship. Putting your hands on a tree will ground you. A tree will connect with your heart and soul and help you relax your emotions. Trees help us to see the magic in our lives.

MOUNTAINS

Mountains have deep symbolism. From the top of a mountain, you see a beautiful vista. Then, you go down the mountain, and you feel blessed and good that you did the climb. In this way, mountains are representative of your earthly journey.

Mountains also support us by their steadfastness. When a mountain appeared in my room as a guide, it gave me a tremendous amount of support and helped me understand the new direction I needed to go in my life.

WATER

Our bodies are approximately 60 percent water, which is why we feel such a strong emotional connection to it. Water is a strong guide and can represent different things. When I'm near water, I am in communication with it on a deep level. It's pulling me in, pushing me away, and sharing secrets with me. We are vibrating together.

A body of water by itself is quite magical, although one aspect I'd like to bring attention to is the energy of a body of water as a source of guidance. Oceans are full of salt, which we know can cleanse us. While rivers are always flowing, so their energy feels new and alive. The location of the body of water and history of it provides guidance as well. Tune into the water and into your feelings, and let the water guide you.

FLOWERS

Flowers are magical guides in the sense of their vibrancy, color, joy, light, and love. Flowers are a guide for us because when we look at them, we have a response—a memory of them, whether good or bad. Therefore, flowers help us understand a little more about our journey on the Earth plane—why we're here, what we're doing, and how we can better direct ourselves.

Flowers have strong energy and are full of color. Color is one of the languages of our soul and a way we can communicate without muddying things up with words or definitions or past experiences. In this way, flowers can speak to the purity of our souls and help us connect with Divine energy.

Put your hand over an open flower. Close your eyes and tune into how you feel. It's a beautiful way to communicate with them.

FORMS IN NATURE

Guides don't have to be in physical form; they can be the shapes of clouds, the color of the sky, or the face of a rock. These magical symbols can open you up to a deeper expression of yourself and help you remember the mystery you are a part of.

Clouds are in constant motion, changing shape and form. When you're seeing something in a cloud, like an angel or an animal, it's not only the cloud, but the form the cloud takes that has importance. And that's what you pay attention to.

Also, notice what you see and whether it turns out to be real or not. Walking through the woods, I will often see guides. I remember walking with a friend, and we both saw an old crone up ahead. She was clear as day. When we got closer to her, we realized it was a tree. Nature shares guidance in this way. It happens all the time.

These profound experiences open you up to the magic and mystery of your life. And so, they're guiding you at that moment to believe something deeper inside yourself.

COLOR

Color is the language of our souls. It is a powerful way for us to deepen our relationship and conversation with our guides. When you have a guide that shows up as color, they get you thinking creatively and help you expand into limitless consciousness.

I had a guide show up in a cloud-type circular shape that was yellow and orange. She invited me to experience what guidance can be like outside the parameters of what we understand. She asked me to expand my awareness for a deeper understanding of what this world is about and to live from a mysterious and magical place.

Our guides want us to step away from the definitions of what people ascribe to specific things and determine our own meanings. When a guide shows up with just color and shape, you must trust your own inner wisdom, guidance, and communication, because there is no representation of that energy out in the world. That's personal to you and it's powerful because you're developing an intimate and individual connection.

NUMBERS

Numbers communicate so much more than their numerical value. Numbers are guides that have their own language—a multidimensional language. To me, the meaning of numbers is infinite. Guides are energy, and numbers are energy, too.

Think about this: How often do you see the same sequence of numbers? If you ask people if they see repetitive numbers, most will say yes, whether they believe in guides or not. Try it, and you will see.

I've been fascinated by numbers since I was a kid. Phone numbers and dates were easy to memorize. I could add, subtract, and do simple multiplication in my head. That has disappeared, with technology being what it is today. Hand me a calculator or let me look up the contacts in my phone. Even though I'm not memorizing numbers the way I used to, they are still talking to me.

When my gifts started opening, I saw the same numbers repeatedly. I knew they were trying to communicate with me but didn't know what they wanted to tell me. The more I opened to my gifts, the more they talked. Now I see numbers as guides. They can be the answer to a question, and they can also guide you. Does that sound strange? Think about it. How would it feel to have your favorite number walking by your side, giving you information about what to do and where to go? To me, that idea sounds quite beguiling.

Each number holds its own distinct energy. I can ask the number 9 about my soul's journey. The number 5 can tell me all about the changes happening in my life. And the number 6—well, the number 6 may point me toward a new community. So, don't write off numbers as just being messages from your guides. Lean into the idea that they are guides themselves. Let them reveal themselves to you.

SOUND

Sound is a guiding principle made of vibrations, and your guides can also show up as vibration. You hear a horn, and you have a feeling about it. There is something it's telling you. Our guides want us to understand that the more "out of the box" we think, the deeper our communication can be with our guides. They're inviting us to recognize that anything can be a guide, because the further we go into the unknown, the more we access information in the known—and the more we get to know ourselves from an inner perspective.

For example, the musical note C has a special meaning for me. I experience it as a guide. When my guides tell me to lean into them, I know that the C note is something I can lean into, and that makes me feel safe. I know to communicate with the C note because it wants to show itself to me.

The universe is the language, the dance, and the symphony. Your guides teach you how to do that dance, play that symphony, and speak that soul language. When you see a sign, is it a nudge from the universe, or are your guides connecting directly with you? There's a vast difference between the universe having your back and you having an intimate relationship with guides that love you and are speaking to you. Those are different worlds.

However, it also depends on your relationship to the universe as God, your source, or your guide. If you feel an intimate connection with the universe as God, your connection may occur that way. It's your unique experience. If you think it's the universe, what's your intimacy with that experience, as opposed to receiving a personal message from your guides? Deepen into the feeling. Which is more intimate for you? What holds you in more awe? That's the answer for you.

For a moment, let's expand into the limitless potential our guides want us to embrace. Because there's no limit, it doesn't have to be that the universe has your back, or that you received a personal message from your guide. It could be both. Sometimes you might hear from the universe and sometimes you might receive a personal message.

People stop their experience when they try to intellectualize it. You can't overthink these experiences. There's an intelligence that comes in, and you don't want to deny that fact. When you have a visceral reaction to something, pay attention. You don't have to figure it out.

Rather, say, "Let me just deepen into this and see how I feel."

It might be your guides or the universe letting you know, *Hey, we're here and we love you.* That's pretty special, too. Now, let's continue and explore ways our guides connect with us.

HOW GUIDES CONNECT WITH US

—————◆—————

We communicate with our guides from our inner awareness—our deep knowing.

"Learn to use your gifts, and it will move your life along." That is what a medium said to me when I was starting to learn about the gifts I had.

Following that advice truly has changed my life. I'd like to take it a step further for you. Learn to communicate with your guides and grow your gifts, and you will enter the ultimate experience of this lifetime. You will change in ways that are deliciously breathtaking; you will invite life in with excitement and experience it with awe. When you connect with your guides and communicate with them using your gifts, your guides will express the meaning of moments, and life will speak through you.

You connect with your guides through your psychic senses: clairvoyance, clairsentience, claircognizance, clairaudience, empathic abilities, and the dream state. They will speak to you by leaning on you, touching you, or whispering. It might feel like a hair falling on you or look like light running past you. Or they will call your name, and you will turn, but no one will be there. They will show you things by bringing your attention to a specific symbol, sound, color, or number. Trust and know that your guides are there. Open your psychic senses and start communicating with them.

My experience with guides is that they come in with a peaceful energy. It is different for everyone because we all feel differently. That's part of what makes us unique. Usually, the feeling of guides won't be an intense emotion like exhilaration or depression and sadness. You may strongly feel their love, but they don't sway you with feeling one way or another. They meet you with an emotional energy that you can respond to.

Everything you feel, hear, see, and sense is information, and you are the instrument through which your guides work. This means that your body, experiences, perceptions, and relationships have meaning for you. Guidance is filtered through your instrument, which helps you discern what's right for you and what doesn't resonate with you. When you bring your consciousness into your physical body, you will feel your guides' energy around you.

Typically, your guides will highlight one psychic gift before they highlight your multitude of gifts, because they want you to develop that first gift and understand how it is working in your own physical being. People used to believe you had to be born with your psychic gifts; however, consciousness is higher these days, and you can open and develop your psychic gifts at any age. You also can reignite gifts you had as a child but shut down because you found they were not accepted, or someone told you they weren't true.

As you explore the diverse ways your guides communicate with you, pay attention. Tune in to your natural tendencies to see what your dominant gifts are. Don't compare yourself to other people.

People will say, "I don't see my guide."

They are feeling their guides—feeling the information—but they negate the feeling because they're so focused on wanting to see someone.

It is important to know what your psychic senses are and how they work so that you can communicate clearly with your guides. Each gift is special—an inner point of view. Your psychic gifts are like a line of energy—an umbilical cord from your soul to your guide. They are the infinite wisdom inside of you, communicating with your guide.

CLAIRVOYANCE

Clairvoyance means "clear seeing," and it's rooted in the third-eye chakra. When you want to open and strengthen your gift of clairvoyance, you want to cultivate a presence in this chakra because of the different ways it can help you to see.

You might see visions in your third eye itself if you close your eyes and go into your third-eye chakra. When I do this, I see it as a room. To me, it has a front, back, and sides, like a room does. It could be circular; it could be square. And you could sit in that room. See yourself sitting in that room while you communicate with your guides in the third-eye chakra. This gives them another way of coming through and speaking with you.

The other way to see them is through third-eye projection. It's not necessarily in the 3-D physical, as if we were sitting in a room together and we saw a bunny rabbit hop by. Spirit might project images from your third eye out into the physical room while you have your eyes open. These are usually one-dimensional images.

Or you could see your guide in the physical, as if it was a person, and they look very 3-D. And you would think they were a person, but they aren't actually there. Physical manifestation in the 3-D is another form of clairvoyance. You see a person standing there; then you turn away, and when you turn back. it's a lamppost—or he is gone.

In another type of clairvoyance, your guides will repeatedly show you a physical symbol that they want you to pay attention to. For example, you are running in the park and notice it is full of squirrels. You may think, *Well, I'm in a park, of course I'm going to see squirrels.*

But your guides made you focus on the squirrels because they're communicating a message to you through that particular physical symbol. It's like being on a great date. Everything else goes out of focus, and all you see are the squirrels.

Light and vibration are other ways of seeing. You can see light out of the corner of your eye or a light that is vibrating. You can see energy vibrating. The energy may take on a cloudy look and then vibrate, or it might take on a certain shape. You might see squiggly lines vibrating.

I saw one type of vibrating energy when I was on a hike. In front of me on the path was a square of squiggly, cloudy lines. It was vibrating energy, and I knew it was a doorway to another dimension. Writing one of my stories for this book, I saw a white light in the middle of the room, as if someone had taken a paintbrush and brushed it there. It had the look that a brush makes on a wall with color. It was big and beautiful. I love seeing things like that. They remind me that I have guidance around me all the time.

CLAIRSENTIENCE

Clairsentience is "clear feeling" or perceiving information through a feeling within your body. It is tied to the third chakra, which is above the navel. It's what we consider our intuition.

It's important to concentrate on where you physically feel things. Your body works as a pendulum. Even without other stimuli, it can sense when something is off or feels good. Remember, your body is your instrument. It will express itself by changing the way it feels. You may feel energetic information in your heart or in your stomach. Your body might start tingling, a signal that you need to pay attention.

Tuning into your body gives you a yes, no, or a neutral answer. You want to learn what each answer feels like. When I get chills in my body, I know it's a confirmation from my guides. When my body starts to shut down, I know it's a no. My throat shuts down, my stomach gets nauseous, and I want to throw up. That's a clear no to me. And then, neutrality is just a neutral feeling; you're not feeling anything. And that's also information from your guides.

CLAIRCOGNIZANCE

Claircognizance is "clear knowing." In a split second, you will get an entire story about something—a download. Claircognizance information will have the feeling of history. There will seem to be a past and a future in it. It has so much. It's a multidimensional experience.

This is why you have to know your instrument. For me, claircognizance drops in the center of my head. You may get your claircognizance in the center of your throat, in your heart, or outside your ear. It doesn't matter where it occurs. It's like a news flash of something you didn't know. You might meet a person and know their whole story within a nanosecond, or get downloads of information from your guides. The information might fill all your psychic senses. These are all forms of claircognizance.

CLAIRAUDIENCE

Clairaudience is "clear hearing." This information is linear and heard as sentences, like the way we talk to each other. It's easy to get confused about which type of information we are receiving. Claircognizance is a download of tons of information. Clairaudience reveals itself sentence by sentence.

There are a variety of ways to hear. You might experience a nudging or a news flash, or you may wake up hearing a song in your head. That is clairaudience.

You could be doing something and all you're hearing is the blower from the gardener, and you think it's just because it's an annoying sound. But then, the sound becomes amplified and the energy behind it grows in intensity. That's clairaudience. Physical sounds are just as important as internal sounds. And like clairvoyance, our guides use our physical environment to get our attention.

A song may pop into your head, and you think, *Oh, I must've just heard it; it's not guidance.*

Your guides have put that song in your head so that you can read the lyrics. Or the song makes you feel a certain way, and your guides are communicating with you through the song. If you think to look up the lyrics and one line jumps out at you, that is a layering of gifts–clairvoyance and clairaudience.

Pay attention to where you hear. You may hear in the center of your head, in your heart, or in your throat. You can hear inside your head, and it may sound like your own voice. My guides speak where my ear meets my face, so I know exactly where to listen.

EMPATHIC ABILITIES

Empathic ability is rooted in your heart chakra. It is active when you physically and emotionally feel energy. It's feeling the emotions of a physical place, an environment, or a person and knowing exactly what they're feeling, *Oh, they're depressed, they're sad, or they're super excited.*

There are various levels of empathic ability. Empaths sometimes also feel physical pain in their body that is energy from someone else. Feeling energy is a psychic ability and another indicator of what you should pay attention to.

Psychometry is a tool for people with empathic ability. Psychometry involves holding an object and feeling the energy from it. For example, I can't have antique objects near me because, I can feel the sadness, the unhappiness, or whatever happened near that object. The object also holds the history of the person who owned it. Just by holding the object, I understand the whole history.

It's important for empaths not to pick up the energy and make it their own. Empathic people can get tripped up if they don't know how to separate from the energy. They might shut down their heart because they can't handle what they're feeling. You never want to shut down your heart because it's your truth center.

Empathic ability is another tool that our guides use to communicate with us. Imagine going into an apartment that you are thinking of renting. You feel heartache in the space. That is your guide letting you know the space's energy may need clearing, because there was deep sorrow in there, and they don't want you moving into a place that has that energy. Or the opposite is true. You walk into an apartment and feel energized and happy. Your guides are letting you know that it's a good place for you. Pay attention to the guidance that comes through your empathic abilities.

DREAMS

Guides will speak to us in our dreams, using all our psychic senses. In the dream space, we are more open, feel more in control, and can use our imagination freely. The blocks we have up during our waking life are gone, blocks that may make us feel fearful if we see a guide show up in our room when we're not ready to see it. In the dream state, our guides have more accessibility to us, and more imagination is at play. Guides can show up physically as ascended beings, animals, or colors—or in any other form.

They will also come through our dream state because, during the day, we're so busy that we often don't pause and take time to communicate with our guides. We want to communicate with them, but we are busy and worried about the dishes and the bills and picking the kids up and whatever life activities keep us in a distracted state.

When you go to sleep at night, you shut down your thoughts and become quiet. That's when your guides inch their way into your dream state. Finding you asleep, your guides can start communicating with you and delivering their messages.

While you sleep, you might have psychological and psychic dreams. In a psychological dream state, you're working on a psychological issue. Sleep turns off your conscious mind and your unconscious mind can rise to the surface and give you information about things you need to work on and heal to move forward.

Psychic dreams occur as a vivid dream state. There are several types of psychic dreams. The most common is precognitive, which is when you have a dream about something that's going to happen in the future. You know it was precognitive information when it happens.

In a psychological dream, you wake up feeling emotional residue and realize you must work through something. In a psychic dream, you wake up with vivid and clear information. When you wake up from a psychic dream, your emotions may be neutral. It feels like you've touched something extraordinary that imparted wisdom to you. Psychic dreams don't leave you with the emotional residue that a psychological dream does.

Sometimes, when you wake up at three in the morning, your guides are waking you up. If you can, allow yourself to wake up, get quiet, breathe with your guides, and see what kind of messages they want to bring forward. If you're feeling anxious or have "monkey brain," allow your guides to nudge you toward something helpful to read or a good video. Usually, it's better to read than to have the screens on at night, but either one can work to bring you incredible information. When this happens to me, my guides wake me up and tell me to search a specific topic on YouTube or read something.

There I find exactly what I need to hear or read. It's the solution that has been eluding me. That is a guided moment through your dreams.

DIVINATION TOOLS

Divination tools can help you open to your gifts and learn how you receive information. Tarot cards, runes, and a pendulum are common divination tools that can become an integral part of your development and expansion. You can use one or more of these tools for the rest of your life or decide, after a time, that you no longer need them.

Pay attention to how you use the tools. Is something jumping out visually? That's clairvoyance. What are you feeling? That's empathic ability. What are you hearing? Even if all you're hearing is the fan from your computer, that's clairaudience. If you immediately know what the message is, that's claircognizance. This is all information to see what your prominent gifts, or "clairs" are, and to understand how you receive information.

As I've said, you have to learn your instrument. Understanding how you are using your psychic senses, as well as how your guides are communicating with you, will help you move through life with more ease.

I like teaching through story because, although you are your own instrument, hearing stories from other people helps you recognize what may be happening to you. When I was opening to my gifts, I received validation when I met someone who shared similar experiences. It made me trust my instrument more to know another person and I shared a common way of communicating. It also helped me open more and give myself permission to develop my relationships with my guides.

I trust that as you read these stories, you will see glimpses of yourself, and the urge to communicate with your guides will grow stronger.

PART TWO

*Mystical Connections to Soul Guides
and Divine Teachers*

*Until you make the unconscious conscious,
it will direct your life and you will call it fate.*

—CARL JUNG

HOME TO MY SOUL

Once again, I feel the pull to leave the place I call home—the apartment where my mediumship skills cracked open, I learned how to channel, spirits appeared, disembodied voices sang out to me, and I developed into a spiritual reader. But now, the walls of this space are closing in on me, trying to contain me, and keeping me from growing further. A familiar feeling of lack of safety leaks into my consciousness. Lack of worthiness sings in the recesses of my soul. Memories from my youth appear.

Things around me become topsy-turvy. New, argumentative neighbors party on their balconies at all hours of the night. When I approach them, they scream profanities at me that even my Brooklyn side fears. Retreating to my bedroom, their voices grow louder as if they are in bed with me. My skin crawls, and my anxiety grows.

I have to get out of here, but how?

I know I am meant for something better than this—meant to live in a peaceful situation. My guides keep telling me I am worthy of more. They want me to find a place I can finally call home. They urge me to spread my wings and take a risk. But my wings feel clipped by memories from my past. Without financial means, I feel trapped.

Growing up, I never really had a home. We grew up in a railroad house with all the rooms connecting to one another. No privacy. The five of us basically slept in one room and shared one bathroom. The place was congested, noisy, and uncomfortable.

My mother got the house after my parents' divorce. Struggling to raise four kids and pay the mortgage by herself, she had little money left to repair the home. My father, though wealthier than us, barely paid child support. He would not give us money to fix the cracked sidewalks, the unstable banister, the drafty halls, and everything else that was in disarray. One neighbor wrote my mother an anonymous letter about how our home was an embarrassment to our block. I felt so bad for my mother. She did the best she could with what she had.

On my twenty-first birthday, my father bought my mother's half of the house. My mother, two of my brothers, and I said good riddance to our childhood home. I felt the crumbling walls of my youth disappear and found a new home.

On my own in Manhattan, I struggled to make a peaceful home. Never fully understanding what the word "home" meant or how it should feel, I talked to my therapist, who suggested enlisting a few friends to help me decorate my apartment and create a haven. It worked. My New York City apartment felt warm and inviting—a place I could finally call home.

As soon as I can breathe, 9/11 happens and my shallow sense of safety quickly gets replaced with fear, anxiety, and doom. I pack up my things and move to Los Angeles. The tragedy of 9/11 catapulted me out of the comfort of my home and into the darkness of the unknown. Lacking safety became an ever-present theme for me.

Now, in my Los Angeles apartment, the shift is happening again. Feeling uncomfortable with the angry neighbors, I turn to my guides for help.

Sitting cross-legged in meditation on my bed, I ask my guides: *How can I buy a home?*

My credit is good, but I am in debt. I lean into my guides.

How can I make this happen?

Ask your father for the money was my guide's loving but challenging answer.

What?! I respond with shock and disbelief, with fear rising in my throat.

He is getting money from selling your childhood home. Ask him for the money.

I knew they were right. He was selling the house I grew up in and was making a huge profit on the sale.

I try to ignore my guides, but they are in every corner, even in conversations with friends, sending me signs and urging me to call and ask him for a down payment. Finally, I give in. I have been working with my guides for five years, and I know I can trust them, so I make the call.

I sit there trembling as my father answers the phone.

My guides whisper in my ear: *Ask him.*

Eventually, I bring the conversation around to the sale of the home and the money he is getting. He shares that he is going to give a large portion to his ex-girlfriend so she can have a home of her own.

Shocked, I respond, "I'd love to have a home, too. Why are you giving it to her?"

"Because she is like a daughter to me."

"But I am your daughter." I am met with silence.

"She needs to have a home. I owe it to her," he says.

"But I need to have a home, and I'm your daughter," I say with courage, launching into a monologue about why he should help me buy one.

He agrees. But we go back and forth on the conditions of him giving me the money, and he tortures me. As weeks go by, our conversations go from me not getting the money to me getting the money. During our volley, my guides insist I search for a home.

I continue to look but struggle to find anything that fits my budget until my guides tell me to go see this ramshackle house that is a short sale. Trusting them, I see the home. It is a mess. I mean a mess! While I navigate a small path around the garbage and clutter, my guides jump up and down.

This is it! This is your home!

They take my attention away from the stained-filled carpets, clutter, and broken-down appliances and put it on the brick fireplace and cathedral ceilings. With my guides' help, I can see the soul of the house and its beauty as I walk through the darkly lit rooms.

I put in an offer, and it is a long and harrowing process because of the owner's circumstances.

Am I going to get this home?

My guides say, *Yes.*

The paperwork is iffy and takes even more time. This is my first home. I want it, and I am scared.

Growing impatient, my father starts bellowing every time we talk: "It's this house or nothing else!"

Clinging to the dream and my guides, I fervently pursue the journey of securing the home. Finally, we close two days before Christmas. Keys in hand, I'm excited to walk through the house. I open the door. With the clutter gone, it looks worse than I thought. Going from room to room, I see mold on the walls and broken windows. It's horrible. Panicked and petrified about what I have just done, I sit down and bawl. I feel so alone.

My guides say, *Trust us.*

Freaking out, I gather the names of contractors and designers, who can help me figure out this mess. The first walk-through with a contractor and designer is a disaster. The designer covers her face with a scarf, afraid to breathe in the air. The contractor looks at me and taps the shower tiles, and the tiles crumble to the ground. He sighs, gives me a verbal quote, and asks if I have the money.

"I'm getting a loan," I respond.

"You can't get a loan that fast. It will take months," he scoffs.

I hear my guides whisper to me: *Get rid of them. You will get the loan.* I usher them out the door.

Straddling crying and excitement for two months, I continue to follow every direction my guides give me. The bank easily and effortlessly gives me a renovation loan. I hire the angel architect who charges me half his usual rate and the contractor who used to be a magician. Sixty days later, I have the most beautiful home I have ever seen—every corner picked out by me. I know exactly what I want because a year prior, my guides had me do a vision board of where I wanted to live—from the green kitchen cabinets to the beautiful granite to the wide wood-plank floors. I have a home, and it's mine.

Then, realization hits. On top of my mortgage, I am now in renovation loan and credit card debt totaling $150,000. Sitting cross-legged in meditation once again, I cry out to my guides.

They respond, *Marilyn, for the next three weeks, you may not think about this debt. Any time it drops in, put your hands up in the air and give it to us.*

By day three of putting my hands in the air, an entire course about teaching people how to communicate with their guides drops into my soul. Excitedly, I get to work on it right away. Two days later, the solution of how to get out of debt drops in. Thirty days later, I teach a live course, which is the first course I ever taught on how to communicate with your guides. I refinance my precious home and am out of debt.

Seven years later, I sell my home for a huge profit, and my guides lead me to my next home—another magical story that I will save for later. I'm so grateful to my dad, who, through all our trials and tribulations, helped me buy my first physical home, and to my guides, who brought me home to my soul.

Marilyn Alauria

FROM BEHIND THE VEIL

Two days before the winter solstice and the ending of the Maya calendar on December 21, 2012, I was 10 days away from the expected birth of my first child.

With the weight of him dropping I felt like he was actively swimming toward his new home. Tired of not being able to bend over to tie my sneakers or wash my feet in the shower, I was restless too. Looking out the window of our home, the nearby lighthouse flashed its green light, inviting me for a walk. The cold wind off the Atlantic welcomed me outside, and as I leaned into it, I felt a sharp and deep pain in my abdomen and low back.

I went back inside to call my partner and my midwife about what might be my first contraction. My midwife insisted I wait for a stretch of close contractions about five minutes apart before heading to the birthing center for a planned water birth. My partner drove while I tried to find a comfortable position for the forty-minute ride. Even though the pain in my back was increasing, I was filled with joy and excitement. A quickening of my heart arose, reminiscent of the anticipation I regularly felt as a runner before a race as if toeing the starting line while simultaneously imagining the finish line tape tearing across my chest.

Determined to have a natural birth, I labored for the next 21 hours. I had two rounds of sterile water injections administered into my back, which felt like fire igniting my skin, but the searing pain in my low back only grew. At 6:30 p.m. the next day, December 20th, I decided I wanted an epidural.

I was devastated to leave behind my midwife who knew me, my body, and my birth plan, and had been such an emotional support for nine months. Before my partner and I crossed the parking lot to the hospital for a traditional birth, I glanced one last time at the birthing pool–the cauldron from which I had thought my son would emerge in an alchemical birth of ease, moving from amniotic fluid to its inviting waters.

An anesthesiologist gave me medicated relief while he talked to me about marathoning and his wife's pursuit of qualifying for Boston. My anxiety eased and I caught my breath again while the medicine flowed into my spine. My new nurse, a kindred spirit with eyes of green that held my gaze, explained what to expect. She told me to rest as much as I could and that, given my state of dilation, it wouldn't be long. The clock on the wall revealed it was now after eight o'clock in the evening.

Almost an hour later, I felt a sudden and enormous pressure. He was ready. The soothing sound of R. Carlos Nakai's flutes playing on my iPod was shattered by the doctor and other staff running in.

"His heart rate is dropping. Get oxygen on her!" screamed the nurse.

"We are going to prepare you for an emergency C-section," she said to me in my terror and confusion. "We need to take him out right now."

With tears flowing, I did the only thing I knew to do—I called on the Goddess Green Tara, a Divine ascended master. Chanting her mantra over the voices of the medical staff, "Om Tare Tuttare Ture Soha," I repeated it like an incantation, a call directly to her. *Please, Green Tara, come, please help me,* I prayed as I looked down at the tattoo of her on my right forearm. For I was a mariner caught in a sudden storm, searching the landscape for her, for the green rays of my island lighthouse to guide me to safety.

The room started spinning, and I became lightheaded. A bright emerald green light flashed in front of my eyes while my nurse's hands appeared with an oxygen mask. I closed my eyes, still seeing the flashing green light behind my eyelids.

"Breathe," she instructed.

The pillows behind my back transformed into the strong arms of the Goddess. Green Tara held me from behind, her legs up at her sides, as I lay against her luminous body. The only sounds I heard were the soft murmur of the medical equipment and the flutes as I let go into her embrace.

"Om Tare Tutarre Ture Soha," I repeated again and again.

Someone began wheeling the bed out of the room, and my heart sank. But just as suddenly, the movement stopped, and the bed reversed back inside.

"His heart rate is normal," someone said. "We can do this here."

I heard a knock. It was my midwife; she had just finished her shift and was watching from the doorway.

"He is coming," she said before telling the doctor and nurse her role.

My midwife held my hand as she and the nurse guided me to push.

My son's head emerged, and my nurse shouted, "Oh my God, he's in his caul! Look! He is in his fully intact caul! I have never seen this."

My partner stared in awe at my son's dark hair flowing inside the perfectly intact water sac surrounding his head as he emerged.

My son came forward with surprising ease. The doctor carefully removed the now partially broken sac around his face and head and placed him on my chest. When I asked about the caul, my midwife explained that this thin membrane containing the amniotic fluid in which the baby grows is rarely intact upon birth.

"He is a caulbearer," she whispered to us.

Leaning over, she explained that caulbearers are thought to be born behind the veil. Magical lore suggests they will never die by drowning and often become midwives due to their ability to work with the Divine, being deeply intuitive and blessed with a healing touch. As I held my son, stunned by the Divine influence on what had transpired, flutes played softly in the background as the mantra of Green Tara echoed in my soul.

Seana Zelazo

BE MINDFUL WHAT YOU ASK FOR

*M*y dad died suddenly of a heart attack, and I didn't get to say goodbye. I have always thought it is better for the living if there is a warning that the end is near. I got the opportunity to feel complete with my mom, but not my dad. After a year of grieving him through all the stages of grief, I still had a nagging feeling, a desire to tell my dad how I felt and what I was going through.

I had been teaching transformational "playshops" around the world and counseling others for many years, so I thought I should be able to get through this more easily. I had the tools to understand the process of moving through the veil and what was on the other side. I knew of my ability to be a conscious channel and trusted my intuition with helping others release their subconscious beliefs, emotions, and spiritual blocks. I knew I would be able to hold space for others through their grief if I could truly reach peace with mine.

Inspired to do a ceremony to connect with him, I lit a white candle and called his name out loud. Staring into the flame, I waited to feel his presence. When I did, I began to tell him all the things I missed about him. I shared my anger, joy, fear, sadness, concern, wonder, and aloneness. I cried and asked questions until I felt complete, and then I asked him to give me a message.

Opening my eyes, I saw the candle's reflection in the window. My closet door started opening slowly. My body felt like it was burning up inside, but my skin was cool to the touch. I knew there was nothing in the closet and I started to think I was having a panic attack.

"Not this way!" I said out loud, fearing he was coming into my body.

Walking to the bathroom mirror and checking my face, I saw no pigment in my skin. I was "white as a ghost." Although I knew I was safe, I trembled. Looking down at the bathroom counter, I saw a picture of my dad. I knew he was trying to speak to me viscerally.

"I know you are here, but I did not want you to come to me this way," I said.

Even though I knew about channeling and was aware of my connection to other dimensions, I had never experienced it like this. I had opened a vortex; although I did not want to be a medium, so I called in my guides to gently escort him out of my space. I lay in bed and vibrated until I fell asleep. When I woke up, I felt a peace and calm I had not known until then. I knew we had connected and that he was the gatekeeper for my newfound ability to channel and leave my body while another energy enters. Allowing this to unfold, I practiced tuning in to other "radio signals" by opening the vortex and going into trance.

Not long after, as I was driving, I had opened a vortex-like funnel, and I felt slammed by all kinds of energies. When I somehow got home and opened the door, my husband had to catch me as I fell out of the car limp and confused. I knew I had to get a handle on this and figure out my boundaries so that I would not be overwhelmed. It took me a couple of years to allow my body to feel the most congruent with the transmissions and to learn that I had control, and I could choose not to allow anyone to come to me anytime they felt like it. Once I learned the protocols and intentionally allowed myself to go out of my body with a laser beam precision and not just open with a funnel approach, it was easier for me to harness the energy and flow.

Why should I keep doing this? I continually asked myself. The answer I knew in my heart. I had asked the Universe to support me in my work for the highest good for all, and if it adds value to humanity, I will continue to be the vessel. I have since trans-channeled a group of teachers from the 5th dimension who call themselves Shamanaste, and I share their guidance with those attracted to this awakening. It was a gift from my dad in an out-of-this-world way.

This experience taught me to be mindful of what I ask the Universe for and be open to the answers received, even though they may not be exactly how I wanted them to occur.

Burge Smith-Lyons

THE EGO'S SURRENDER TO THE DIVINE

Staring at loops of beige carpet on my bedroom floor, my mind swirled with thoughts of suicide. At fourteen years old, hopelessness filled every cell of my being as I envisioned the ways I would end my life. Suddenly, I heard a gentle voice deep within my mind protest, telling me I would get through this dark period of my life and eventually be happy. This quiet, kind voice warned me that if I did end my life in the way I imagined, I would possibly return in a form with even deeper suffering. Though I had never learned about reincarnation or heard voices in my head before, I felt reassured and agreed to endure life hoping the voice was right.

Twenty-five years later, I stood at the pinnacle of success with a high-powered media career, a thriving medical center, and a modicum of celebrity status. I had what most people considered the necessary ingredients for happiness: financial abundance, good health, a beautiful home, a fancy car, and popularity. Still, none of it held any meaning for me.

Smiling on the covers of magazines and appearing bubbly on TV shows, I wore a happy mask while depression loomed within me, never to be seen by even the people closest to me. On the verge of burnout, I once again longed for a way out. But I remembered my agreement to that voice—suicide was not an option.

During an impromptu vacation to the South of France, I shunned my title and status in American media and embarked on an adventure of self-discovery that landed me on stage in a chic nightclub in St. Tropez. Singing and dancing with a crowd of people I didn't know and would never see again, I felt liberated, seen, and unconditionally loved and accepted.

The next morning, as I marveled at the memory of the night before, my reverie ended abruptly when I remembered I'd return to my bleak existence back in America in just two short days. Hopelessness enveloped my body in a dark mist of depression once again.

I flung myself on the bed, shaking, sobbing, and began pleading for God to take my life. "I can't live like this anymore! Take my life, God! Take my body, my mind, my talents, my business. I don't know what I'm doing with them anyway!" A moment of surrender allowed my trembling body to melt into the bed, dissolving the boundaries between "me" and my surroundings.

Though my eyes were closed, a bright white light filled the room. Squinting to find its source, I was shocked to discover it was coming from within my head. Within a second of realizing this, I felt myself being drawn into the light. Leaving my body behind and floating upward, I felt weightless, peaceful, and curious. My tears subsided and I felt gratitude that God was answering my prayer by taking my life. Willingly, I let go.

Through a tunnel of darkness, I arrived at "the other side," where I felt complete bliss. In what felt like a nanosecond, I was shown a vision of my entire life, allowing me to see how each decision, whether consciously made or not, led me to depression.

The presence of a peaceful, wise being arrived at my side and showed me a glowing ball of light, like the sun, which I knew to be the Source of our consciousness. Little droplets of that light, which I saw as souls, descended to earth, infusing the human form with life. The guide showed me that when we incarnate it is up to each soul to discover and declare their purpose, not for our paths to be forced upon us by parents, society, or the media.

"I didn't know I could choose," I said. "If that's the case, I would go back and choose differently."

Immediately, I was shown a new vision of my future where I walked gleefully hand in hand with a child by the Mediterranean Sea. It was clear to me that I lived in France, I was singing professionally, and I was able to heal with my hands. This last point struck me as odd and slightly objectionable, but since I seemed genuinely happy and vibrant in that vision, I said yes to life.

Filled with a sense of wonder and joy, I swiftly descended back into my body. When I opened my eyes, the dark, depressive feeling was gone, and for the first time in my life, I was optimistic about my future.

A few years later, I left America with my young daughter by my side. After one year of living in France, I was singing professionally at live events and recording songs with musicians. I even learned with the help of a Zhineng Qigong teacher how to heal with my hands. The Divine continues guiding me on my path, reminding me to live authentically and wholeheartedly.

Dr. Andrea Pennington

A WAY OF GRATITUDE AND RESPECT

Standing at the bus stop, irritable at having just missed the last bus, I scowled at the world. Unable to see anything in my day to be grateful for, the blustery gray day matched my mood perfectly.

I buried my chin deep into the collar of my coat to keep the cold Alberta wind from chafing my skin. Things couldn't get any worse—or so I thought until I spotted an elderly aboriginal man coming toward me, swaying from side to side like he'd had a couple drinks. Since childhood, I felt nervous around inebriated males. My fear of violence was based on my Irish upbringing, seeing men fight after leaving the pub at night.

Bracing myself for his approach, I noticed a second younger man walking behind him. The second one approached and asked if I had a cigarette to spare. I told him I did not and offered him some money so he could buy some, but he refused.

"I don't need money, I need a smoke," he replied, catching me off guard.

He began asking questions, wanting to know where I came from, where I was going, where I was born, and why I wore lipstick. There was something different about his eyes; they had fire, a spark of some kind. Having discovered

I grew up in Dublin, Ireland, he told me how much he liked the Irish. How great they were as warriors.

"Not afraid to fight," he said, looking deep into my eyes as if addressing my soul. I sensed he also "knew" how ashamed I was of the fighting Irish part of my heritage.

Feeling uncomfortable with the conversation, he began to smile a knowing smile. He shared his good fortune at having a wonderful Irish friend with whom he enjoyed many great fights and many victories. Again, that smile; his amusement was obvious.

Without the courage to say I hated the fighting part of the Irish, I pretended to agree, but I knew he was aware of my deception. After what seemed like an eternity, he told me the elderly man was his father and he should go find him. Reaching up with his hand, he gently touched my face. His skin was like silk, love emanating from his fingertips.

The vibration in my body increased rapidly as I saw him surrounded with light. The love from him washed through me, filling me with peace. He said goodbye and walked away, but after a few steps, he came back. Looking deep into my eyes, he touched the other side of my face. Again, the feel of silk on my skin as the light surrounded him and love washed through me. Smiling, he told me never to be ashamed of myself in any way, that I should honor all that I am as well as everyone I meet along my path. Then he was gone.

A song of joy played in my heart as I walked toward the city center, grateful to be alive. As I walked, visions and ancient wisdom dropped in, showing me that the aboriginal people could not live as we do. Their very nature was different. I saw images of beautiful aboriginal men, women, and children living free and happy lives, aligned with nature, moving across the land in tune with the seasons. Warriors, proud and strong, riding tall and unafraid. Women and children happy and smiling.

It was an awakening and humbling experience presented by a beautiful spiritual teacher dressed as an unemployed aboriginal person. Awareness along with personal embarrassment tore through me. I had judged their drinking and ways of being as negative. Now I saw how imprisoned they must feel in the concrete world we have created. With compassion and understanding, I felt a sense of loss around a way of life more peaceful and respectful of nature. A sacred way that thanked the earth, sun, moon, and Spirit for everything they used. I saw that our way was not necessarily the best or the only way to live. With this lesson, I was able to receive the gift of the warrior energy of my own Irish heritage.

Feeling grateful for and blessed by this experience, I promised myself I would always remember that everything is not always as it seems and that I don't know what is best for others.

Patrishe Maxwell

HEALING ARMS

While working with a client, my eyes closed to better "see" what they were experiencing on a spiritual and energetic level, I saw something bright to the right of my vision. Turning my head, I peeked through slightly open eyelids to get a better look, but nothing was there. Closing my eyes again, I was stunned to see an image of a right arm made of white light. I opened my eyes again but saw only my arms in front of me. One more closing of the eyes, and the powerfully lit up right arm became clear. Looking to the left, I saw an image of an arm of light on that side too, though it was slightly dimmer. Despite being confused by this, I was in awe, vibrating with excitement and a desire to understand what it meant.

I soon learned that the OverLighting Deva of Healing was working with me and through me and wanted to share the images of the arms with me. Not only did I now have this unexpected gift of support, but as I accepted this guide into my life, a previous pain in my hands that made it difficult to hold things and even drive began to lift. Now when my hands get warm, I know the OverLighting Deva of Healing is within me or near me, guiding me on a benevolent path to act for the highest good of all involved. She not only assists with the laying on of hands, but provides an energy pull or an intuitive hit when someone needs healing.

As I stood in the buffet line at a conference in 2019, I recognized this sensation and began looking around. Without an obvious person in need, I sat at a table with a few empty spots and started into a conversation that yielded no energy hits.

I had almost forgotten the pull until I went to use the restroom and two women entered. There it was—the hands activating and the sense of knowing. While washing my hands, I naturally became a part of their conversation.

We were all at the same conference, confirming the energy pull I had felt earlier at the buffet. I could feel the emotions of one of the women and asked if I could say something a little off the wall to her. While asking about her childhood dog she revealed that her dad had the dog put down, and I sensed the emotions from that trauma were still tied to her behavior in her adult life. In a few short moments of conversation, and with the Deva's assistance, she had an emotional release of related anger and sadness.

The OverLighting Deva guides me to recognize the energy around me more deeply and is steadfastly there with me throughout pivotal moments of helping myself and others. My first experience of the Deva involved her lighting up my healing arms, but I have also learned she is behind the colors I see when I close my eyes during healing sessions, continually serving as a healing source that helps light up the world.

Sandra Pelley

ENCOUNTER WITH YOGANANDA

elieving I could deepen my connection with the Divine through denial of earthly needs, I fasted for several days before receiving darshan, a blessing through spiritual contact from the presence of gurus, living masters, and God-realized beings.

During a meditation the morning after receiving darshan, the spirit of Paramahansa Yogananda visited me. Vibrating in a heightened state of awareness, contemplating my hunger for God versus my hunger for food, he came right into my field of awareness and joyfully introduced himself. His presence was so clear and discernible, I thought he might materialize. Hovering above the ground in a lotus posture, I could even perceive him slightly with my physical eyes, though the image in my mind was stronger.

His levity was already rubbing off on me as I engaged him with questions and joked that he had come to lighten my spiritual teacher's workload. He smiled, and as he began to share the radiant glow of his love, I became more aware of a lack of self-love that I had been feeling. The contrast between Yogananda's mastery and my imperfections glared in my self-awareness.

Yogananda touched on a great dilemma I could not ignore. Although I had passion for following Spirit and living the teachings of Christ and the

Ascended Masters, a part of me wondered how I could ever overcome the mistakes of my past, including past lives, to become a radiant being like the Masters. As I felt the weight of regret, Yogananda read my thoughts and began to laugh. Shaking me out of my despair, he explained that the path of enlightenment is fairly predictable and a great many people feel the same way when they reach a point of deepening commitment.

If only you knew how many mistakes I and other Masters made in our lives leading up to our enlightenment, you would not feel so bad, he said. It is common, once you begin to cultivate a closer relationship with the Masters, to become more critical of your faults, but the complex entanglements we can experience with the unresolved memories of the past are really just an issue of self-love.

Yogananda then gifted me with some of the strength of his self-love and the knowledge he, too, once felt his mistakes were an insurmountable obstacle to his growth. His insights resonated through the whole of my being, and I saw through his eyes what I had been doing to myself. Wanting to change or discard the parts of me that I did not love or accept only reinforced a feeling of separation from love. In this pivotal moment, my self-imposed exile from God's unconditional love shifted.

I no longer believed I had to achieve the radiant levels of mastery I aspired to on my own. Yogananda was demonstrating how we could receive much of what we need as a direct transference from the Masters as a kind of spiritual inheritance. This consciousness of self-love that enveloped me was part of Yogananda's darshan.

Nobody walks the path of enlightenment alone, he explained. Everyone on this journey is promised the help of those who have crossed such thresholds before. This is the way it has been done for millions of years.

I shared that I hadn't heard from the Masters as much lately—at least not as much as I did some years ago.

Have I done something wrong or gotten off track? I asked.

He responded by assuring me I hadn't done anything wrong, but that I was being given a break to enjoy life.

Enjoy these periods when they come, he said, *because on the other side, you will be much busier.*

My body relaxed with a new understanding that I didn't have to try so hard to fulfill the mission all the time.

Why not do something celebratory to break your fast? he suggested.

In that moment, my guides conveyed that I did not need extreme feats of abstaining from earthly things to get closer to the Divine. I had passed the test of developing such discipline. Now it was time to allow Spirit to commune with me through the earthly experience. That day, I celebrated food and being human, with an understanding that our imperfections are invitations to deepen our self-love.

Saryon Michael White

UNEXPECTED PACKAGES

My guides come in unexpected packages. One is about three feet eight inches tall, with dirty blonde, chin-length curly hair, a tuft of which sits over her forehead as she grows it out from her bangs experiment. The other is three feet of pure muscle, with shorter but still wild dirty blonde hair. We were blessed with our girl late on Christmas day and our boy two and a half years later. I didn't know in those moments that Spirit would use them to guide me back to wholeness.

It was a sunny Friday in mid-May, the kind of day that reassures us Wisconsinites that winter is officially behind us. My daughter ran to her classroom with a friend, and I walked my son to his. As I stood in the doorway saying goodbye, this almost three-year-old tightly hugged my leg. After a minute or so, he took an apprehensive step back, then ran and clung back on. This went on for a few minutes before the teacher peeled him away. As I took that opportunity to disappear out the door, I saw his face start to crinkle and his mouth open, the first sounds of his cry coming through just as the door shut behind me.

That breaks my heart every time, I thought, as I walked away. Then I remembered my lesson from a healer and shaman just the day before: *Don't stop there, follow the feeling.*

Driving away, I asked myself when the first time was that I felt a broken heart. In my mind's eye, I saw a glimpse of a little girl reaching up for an adult and feeling rejected; a little girl who in that moment wanted physical comfort and didn't get it. That little girl was me.

Then it hit me—my son is helping reflect some of my deep, buried wounds. Even though he's getting heavy, I love picking my son up and snuggling with him. The way he wraps his arms and legs around me and puts his head on my shoulder feels like pure, unconditional love expressed in the physical. A few days before as I bent over to pick him up, I realized I was doing it out of an internal, unconscious "ping" within myself. When I investigated that "ping," I knew it was something in my energy asking for physical love and connection, which I was feeding through a connection with my son. Here I had been thinking I was holding him to show him love, when in fact, I was reaching out to him from a place of lack within myself.

Bringing myself back to the driver's seat heading home, I imagined picking up my little child self and telling her I loved her.

When I got home, I grabbed my mala beads and sat on my back deck for meditation and journaling. This is my favorite spot in the house when our Midwest weather allows me to be outside. Right off our back deck are tall, skinny pine and oak trees that are almost always blowing in the wind. Between their rustling leaves, the birds, and the frogs, I have the perfect nature-filled audio for inner contemplation.

Sitting cross-legged on the blue cushion, I wrapped my amethyst and lapis lazuli mala around my hands, and faced the trees, where the sun was starting to shine through. I recalled the feeling of my broken heart and used a phrase from a spiritual teacher: *I allow this to move through me as quickly and gently as possible.*

I sat quietly for a while, feeling myself release that old energy. As I opened my eyes and picked up my pen to start reflecting on my morning, another insight hit me: This isn't just about me nurturing my little child self. In dropped the insight from another spiritual teacher who said, *The main relationship we need to nurture is between us and our higher selves.*

I realized that my higher self was reaching out to me through my son, asking me to nurture my relationship with her. My former image of a little girl reaching up to an adult was replaced with an image of me reaching up to my higher self when I was yearning for support and connection. Just that morning, I started listening to a podcast about our higher selves as guides and I was thinking I should cultivate that relationship more. Message received.

A month went by. I'd been connecting with my higher self, more and more but hadn't given much attention to my little child self. One night, I was sitting at the dinner table while the kids played in the living room. My son had just started "fomastics," and was showing us how he'd learned to do a flip over a bar. As he was upside-down on the bar on my mini trampoline, my well-meaning daughter started helping him over. He told her to stop, which prompted me to ask her to leave him alone. She kept pushing.

Finally, I yelled, "Just listen to me!" which sent that beautiful, sensitive soul crying to her room.

With sadness coming over me because of how I made her feel, I took that same journal and sat in that same spot on the back deck, facing the trees. Closing my eyes, I took a few deep breaths and brought the situation back to my awareness. It didn't take me long to realize that yelling at my daughter to "Just listen to me!" was my little child self, yelling at me to listen to her. She's been asking for cartwheels and ice cream, and I've been ignoring her pleas to add a little fun and whimsy to my life.

Right away, I asked her what she wanted, and she told me she wanted a popsicle. I opened the freezer and got her a frozen strawberry popsicle, enjoying it on the back deck in the hot summer sun. Through the window,

I heard my surprised husband comment to the kids how weird it was that mommy was eating a popsicle. Between me, my higher self, and my little child self, I suspect this is just the beginning of our beautiful story—and probably a lot more ice cream.

Andrea Andree

CONNECTING TO TIMELESS WISDOM

n November of 2019, I was invited to co-moderate a panel the following January at my old alma mater with a professor of neuroscience and a prominent figure in alternative medicine. This was the opportunity of a lifetime, and I was ready to seize it.

That same week, I received an opportunity to host a TV show on a new network that had launched the week before. I saw it as a sign from the universe. I had never hosted a TV show before, nor had I co-moderated a panel of this magnitude, so I did the only thing I could do, I trusted it would all work out.

A few weeks after accepting both opportunities, I had an idea—what if I offered the panelists a chance to join me for an interview on my new TV show? As far-fetched an idea as it seemed at the time, I mustered up all of my courage and called my friend who was planning the panel event and told her I had saved the two panelists a slot on my show if they were interested. A few minutes later, she confirmed their attendance.

What began as a one-time episode rapidly grew into an ongoing series. By December, I had hosted numerous episodes with my two special guests, and that evening we were going to resume our recordings and dive into an episode on quantum physics and special relativity.

I always arduously prepared for each interview by reading all the books I could find on the subject matter, in this case on quantum physics, science, and spirituality. Despite my research, on that chilly morning I felt inadequate. I felt like a failure, not qualified to facilitate a conversation on quantum physics as I had never even taken a standard physics class in college. So, I asked God for help.

"God," I humbly began, "I need your help please. I am doing this interview tonight and I don't feel qualified or prepared for it and I don't know what to do."

After a beat of silence, God responded, *Ask Einstein.*

"What?" I exclaimed, perplexed.

Once more, after another beat, God responded, *Ask Einstein. One hour before your show, go into a meditative state and ask Einstein for help and he will guide you for tonight's interview.*

An hour before the show began, I sat quietly, silently reciting my Transcendental Meditation mantra, and about ten minutes in, when I was in a deeply peaceful state, I reached out into the abyss and cautiously asked from my heart to the universe, "Einstein, um, I am here on earth and God asked me to reach out to you for help for an interview I'm doing this evening for a show on special relativity and quantum physics. Can you please help?"

In a moment, I felt a counterclockwise swirling energy envelope me. Einstein replied that he was here, and that *Yes,* he could help, but that first I would need to let go and not be afraid. There was only a moment's hesitation before I surrendered, allowing myself to free-fall headfirst, as if going down the spacetime rabbit hole, swirling counterclockwise through the universe.

Whether Einstein and I were gone ten minutes or thirty, I don't recall. I have a vague recollection of him showing me the secrets of the universe—how it was designed and where special relativity came from. Enthralled by what I was experiencing during this journey, I was reluctant to return to do the interview at all. Eventually, Einstein bid me farewell, letting me know he was free anytime I needed help again.

Later that night, at ten o'clock, I recorded our episode. It was clear to me that I was not the one conducting the interview, but rather I was a conduit for the wisdom and insights of Einstein and Source to pour through me.

Jennifer K. Hill

IF ONLY I BELIEVED

They say some of the most fervent prayers evolve from heartfelt tears. As the space empties of clutter, you can hear the Divine whisper. If you believe. But I was a non-believer, eager to push through life doing everything on my own, a plan that had long expired and begged to be rewritten.

For me, God no longer took on the image of an old man with a long, white beard, nor did I see angels as ethereal winged messengers. Those images remained in the good old days when my innocence had nothing better to do than imagine and pretend. I had no time for this now; life was calling me to work. But I struggled.

My favorite elm tree beckoned me to sit under its leafy canopy. With a safe little nest to roost in, it provided cool shade from the scorching sun where I could sob tears of deep yearning. I needed to receive all that I'd given others—to be lovingly supported, deeply seen, heard, and valued. I often wondered what it would be like to be one of my massage clients walking out of my clinic clad in love. I wanted someone to wave their magic wand and make this happen for me too.

A dear friend gifted me a massage voucher to a little aromatherapy boutique I had often passed, and without hesitation, I booked an appointment. Something didn't feel quite right though.

Oh, it's probably my imagination, I told myself, disregarding the whispers in my head.

A distant voice persisted, trying desperately to crack through the airwaves. With a strong message to share, my body became its vehicle. The subtle glitch in my solar plexus that I now recognize as a "no-go zone" bothered me. But my body hungered for a slow, tender massage and I was going to have it. I could already feel the long strokes and warm oil my body so deeply craved.

But Spirit had other plans.

Highlighted by the bright morning sun streaming through the window, a large lizard lounged on the carpet at the bottom of the staircase. Hearing my footsteps, it turned and looked up, its beady eyes peering directly into mine.

Look at me! it called out silently from the spotlight. *Take note.*

Under the thick blanket of fear and self-loathing, I couldn't hear its words.

Occasionally I saw small skinks in the suburbs, but this was a large specimen, the kind you discover in country areas and warmer climates. Mesmerized and dumbfounded, I froze. Where did it come from? How did it enter our home? No doors or windows were open. It couldn't have crawled in through the space under the door. It was far too big.

"Come and have a look at this!" I turned excitedly, calling my husband. When I twisted back, it was gone. It simply vanished.

I mentioned this mysterious encounter to a friend.

"Take note!" she excitedly exclaimed, citing the lizard's significance in aboriginal dreamtime. "It's ancient and comes with a message. Listen!" she urged, but I still struggled to see beyond our odd conversation.

The little aromatherapy shop was scented with my favorite concoction of lavender, bergamot, and sandalwood. Dancing around my nostrils, it enticed me in to explore the shelves. A fountain of trickling water and soft background music convinced me I was in the right place. It was a warm welcome and a promise of things to come.

A loud, croaky male voice unexpectedly shattered the calm with two simple words. "Lizard oil!" he declared. His commanding voice whisking me away from the peaceful environment, momentarily suspending me in a time warp.

"Lizard oil? What's that?" the receptionist snapped, not having time to compose herself.

"It's a very, very important oil," he continued in a distinct indigenous accent. "It heals many things."

Curious to see the face behind the voice, I stopped browsing and turned in the man's direction. Not the typical customer found in an aromatherapy boutique, he lent a sharp contrast to the otherwise petite clientele. Large and barefoot, his long, dark, unkempt hair flowed over his shoulders and partially down his bare tattooed arms.

"Well," the receptionist sniggered as she haughtily examined the man, desperately trying to suppress her laughter. "You won't find any of that here," she emphasized and then repeated it slowly just in case he wasn't able to grasp it the first time.

He turned to leave, and like the lizard, his intense and warm, dark brown eyes looked deeply into mine and twinkled: *Listen carefully.* Allowing judgment to get the better of me too, I momentarily turned to cover my amusement.

The little bell chimed as he opened the door to leave, and like his shadow, I followed to watch him walk away, but he had completely vanished. Looking in both directions and searching the other side of the road, I found only empty sidewalks. There were no cars that would have blocked him from view and no corners he could have ducked behind. He was gone. I returned to the warm, scented clinic but couldn't shake the imprint of his deep gaze.

"Vivian will see you now," the receptionist interrupted my thoughts.

The session began with questions, and thirty-five minutes later, we were still talking. I began to wonder where the massage and nurturing was. Where were the warm towels, the aromatic oils, and the gentle touch that aromatherapy promised to deliver? When the session was finished, I walked out the door. Anger rose from my solar plexus, its heat turning a deep shade of crimson as it reached my face.

"Are you okay?" asked the receptionist whose pompous attitude from an hour before was replaced by loving concern.

"I understand," she empathized as she listened intently to my answer. "Aromatherapy has different arms," she clarified. "One of them is massage, but you'll have to see someone else if that's what you're after. Vivian only works with the psychological and medicinal side of it."

Handing over my dues, I left with a richer understanding of this powerful healing art but ravenous for touch.

The highly unusual events of the day unfolded as I wrote in my journal that night. The dots joined and the absurd experiences began to make sense, illuminating the importance of taking heed. While my body craved to be touched, I was guided to find my solace elsewhere. That night I learned the truth: I am loved, deeply seen, heard, valued, and never alone. I am always protected, supported, and guided. If only I believed.

Yaelle Schwarcz

VOICE ON THE MOUNTAIN

It was late August when I arrived in Ladakh, India, but when the sun goes down in that northern region of the Himalayan Mountains it can get quite chilly. I had just arrived that morning and was staying in the guesthouse attached to Thiksey Monastery. Excitedly, I wrapped myself up to go out to see my first Himalayan night sky. I have a special affinity for Orion's Belt but had purposely not looked up where it would be in the sky when I arrived because I wanted it to be a surprise. Unprepared for how many stars I would see, I never imagined it would be so hard to find Orion. At last, I found him sitting near the western ridge, low in the sky.

I don't know what I expected to happen in that moment. After years of planning this trip, and the built-up anticipation, perhaps I had expected a giant starlit chariot flashing across the sky to welcome me. Or at least a heavenly choir heralding my arrival. Completely worn out from traveling two full days from Sarasota, Florida, I sat there in the dark and realized I had expected something truly magical to take place the moment I got there. Suddenly, I felt small, insignificant, and disappointed.

The next morning, I was up early and immersed in the early morning puja of the monks chanting in Sanskrit. The vibration was transformative and helped to soothe my restlessness. Two hours later my morning exploration continued as I climbed the vast stairs that took me to the Green Tara Temple. Standing outside the entrance, I removed my shoes, and carefully and quietly stepped inside. Completely alone inside the small and beautiful temple, I absorbed the energy as it radiated a feeling of waiting, patience, and acceptance. The walls were filled with images of Green Tara in green and gold, with statuettes placed on small shelves and in glass cases. There were dozens of silk and cotton katas draped around the various forms, perhaps even hundreds, each one a prayer and an offering to the Goddess. I sat cross-legged on the cold stone floor with my back against the cool wall and stared at the central figure—the largest of the images of Green Tara in the temple—in all her simple, yet refined elegance. She looked back at me with that little smile on her face. I found myself crying and wondering why I was there. *Why had I traveled so far? Why had I trusted this trail of breadcrumbs that led me here? What was I supposed to do now?*

My heart cried out, *Don't you know that I am here?*

In the complete stillness of that sacred space, I heard a gentle but firm voice in my heart, *Do you really think that in all of our Infinite Wisdom that we do not know you are here?*

I felt the voice more than I heard it, and I was instantly humbled. There was love, kindness, and acceptance in the voice, but a great strength and power behind it too.

I had come to India in search of the Masters, and here they were, talking to me, comforting me, and lightly admonishing me. In awe to be in their presence, I crumbled before the Divine semblance of God, crying with a mixture of joy and humility.

How could I have doubted? How could I have inwardly railed against the gods the previous night, demanding answers, and expecting instant results?

Finally, I sat quietly, asking for forgiveness, and praying that I would be understood in my naiveté, exhaustion, and desperation for answers.

I thought about the last three years of working full time, squirreling away my pennies to pay for this trip while helping take care of my father who had Parkinson disease. I jumped through every hoop to get here, diligently following the breadcrumbs laid before me. Each vision, each sign, each token became a precious piece of the puzzle, from shamanic journeys to "coincidental" meetings with people to crystal skulls and rocks with fissures in them that matched the same ridgeline as Stok Kangri, the most famous mountain in Ladakh.

Nine months before my departure, one of my teachers and good friends introduced me to Green Tara. She had received a Green Tara ring from her lama and mentor eight years prior who told her that one day she would know when it was time to pass the ring on. In meditation, she received the message that I was the next carrier of the Green Tara ring. She wanted me to have the ring well before my trip so that I could become familiar with Green Tara and begin developing a relationship with her. Two weeks before I left the country, I found out about the Green Tara Temple that is built into Thiksey Monastery.

On that second morning in Ladakh, as I sat in that perfect stillness in the temple, I felt a presence so powerful, so loving, and so kind, that I felt my heart open wide. This voice, this presence, was now a part of me.

Then I heard my instructions: *Relax. Slow down. Get to know the people, get to know the area and the culture. And have fun.*

Taking a deep breath, I understood that by doing as I was told, I would find my answers along the way. From that moment on, I realized the answers were not going to come in a blaze of glory, but rather in the simple experience of being there and being present in each moment. The answers were inside of me, and they always had been. I just needed to listen and allow that knowing to come forward.

On my last full day in Ladakh, I took a long walk to the neighboring village of Shey where there is an ancient abandoned palace now in ruins. Hiking up the side of the mountain above the palace and past the fluttering prayer flags, I found a secluded spot on the side of the mountain facing Stok Kangri in the distance. In the past three weeks, I had plenty of opportunities to sit in meditation with Stok Kangri in the background, and now I wanted to spend one last afternoon with it. In that moment, I heard the voice say, *Now,* and felt the impulse to do a ceremony in honor of the mountain, the land, and the people who cared for it, and also for myself for having the courage to follow my inner guidance that had brought me here. Before leaving, I built a small cairn on the side of the mountain in honor of the Masters who carefully watched over me and guided me on my journey.

On my way back to Thiksey Monastery, I walked along a back dirt road that took me past small farms. The only sounds I heard were the occasional cows lowing, birds twittering, and my sneakers on the gravel. I stopped and just listened to the air around me, feeling the sun on my face, and I realized I had done it—I had followed the instructions given to me that morning in the Green Tara Temple. Not only was I physically moving slower as I meandered down the road, but everything about me had slowed down. I had spent the past three weeks meeting wonderful people who shared their food and beverages with me, strangers who invited me into their homes for tea, including a mother who cried while telling me about her son she had lost in a car accident the year before. I met other travelers who shared their stories about the Masters, and I visited many monasteries in various villages spread far and wide, listening to pujas and absorbing the vibration of the land. I sat at the base of the huge stupas at the monastery seeing the Milky Way with my naked eyes and listening to the tiny bells tinkling as they caught the light winds, like the sound of the cosmos. I stood in the cave of an ancient lama who had once lived there full time, long ago, and felt the power of his energy imprint in the stones around me.

I climbed up Green Tara Mountain in Nubra Valley, a mountain not listed on any map by that name, but the locals call it that. On the side of that mountain the voice of the Masters had joined me again, encouraging me to keep climbing higher. Every time I thought that I was as high as I could go, I heard, *Go higher.* And I did. Each time, I was rewarded with the sight of a beautiful rock formation, or a circle of stones, cairns, and a magnificent rainbow that spanned the valley when I looked back to see where I had climbed from. The Masters told me which stones to collect to bring home with me and I dutifully packed them in my backpack for safe keeping.

Nearly seven years later, I am still on this journey, and every once in a while, I hear the whisper of the Masters, the voice on the mountain. When little things reveal themselves to me, I know the seed was planted in India. I know that the Masters are always with me, and I don't need to travel far to find them.

Christy Perry

YOU GOTTA HAVE FAITH

Contemplating leaving my marriage of 25 years was a decision I did not make lightly. Yet I knew I was unhappy and so was my husband. Life was no longer working for us as a couple. I wanted more, not necessarily a divorce, just more. From the outside, everything looked perfect, but on the inside, I was crumbling.

After much searching, an apartment in an unfamiliar area of Boston became available to rent. This rental would give me time to evaluate who I was and what I wanted out of life and my marriage. Time to be and to think.

Much trepidation and the unknown had me questioning my decision. Fear crept in. My mind could not fully grasp leaving the comfort of the beautiful home I created, nor could my family. Needing guidance to move forward, I asked the Universe to give me a sign to validate that I was making the right decision.

It was the quintessential autumn day in New England. The air was crisp as the afternoon sun streamed through the leaves of the tree-lined street, making the red, orange, yellow, and green leaves glow around me. Signing a year lease for this two-bedroom, two-story apartment with a balcony and dedicated parking space had me feeling overwhelmed, quiet, and subdued.

Questioning my motives, I wondered, *Do I know what the hell I'm doing?* On the other hand, I felt excited to begin again, curious to see how life would unfold. I asked for a sign to know I was making the right decision.

Walking and contemplating my next move, I realized I had 30 minutes before signing the lease. A coffee shop across the street caught my attention. The friendly woman behind the counter and I conversed about the neighborhood. I peppered her with questions.

"Are you the owner of the coffee shop? How long have you been here? Is this neighborhood safe? Do people seem friendly?"

She answered all my questions with patience and kindness, understanding how a big move could be empowering and fearful. With no other coffee shops in this area and the safe feeling of the neighborhood, she and her daughter decided to lease the space six months prior. With a friendly, diverse crowd coming in every day, always sharing pleasantries, she felt good about the area.

After a few more minutes, I thanked her and shared my name. She introduced herself as Faith. I knew right away her unique name was my sign and exactly the feeling I needed to move forward into the unknown.

What I knew for sure was that I wanted something different. I was willing to explore and ask for what I needed despite how unsettling it felt. A new area to explore, walk around, and restaurants to dine in felt more exciting than scary. I signed the lease with ease.

The area proved to be safe, fun, and walkable to a diverse selection of stores and a variety of restaurants with creative, delicious food that kept me occupied. The other tenants became fast friends. My decision, although tough was the correct one. The coffee shop with Faith became one of my favorite places.

Susan B. Mercer

THE VISITOR

When my parents divorced, it was decided they would rotate the holidays. If my sister and I spent Thanksgiving with our mother, we would spend Christmas with our father and visa-versa. The year I turned 12, we spent Christmas with our dad.

My dad was a big kid when it came to Christmas. He and my stepmother always made the house look beautiful. The tree lights burned brightly, including my favorite old-fashioned bubble lights where the heat of the lights made the liquid inside bubble like water on the stove. Somehow it made the tree seem alive. Holly berry lights decorated the entrance from the living room to the dining room. A Christmas "town" was laid out under the tree, each little building emitting its own glow.

Depending on where Christmas fell during the week, we'd usually have a day or two in Long Island before Christmas Day. My stepmother's birthday fell on the 23rd and I loved when we got the chance to celebrate with her in person. We'd spend the days leading up to Christmas making cookies, watching movies, playing games, and if we could brave the cold, taking walks along the beach. Winter in Long Island had a completely different vibe from the summer. Back then, very few people lived in the community all year long, and after Labor Day, what used to be a bustling community of families enjoying summer vacation turned into a virtual ghost town. With most of the houses left empty, it was a bit eerie.

This year on Christmas Eve, I could feel my breathing getting more and more shallow. I had been living with asthma since I was about eight years old, although at the time it was not properly diagnosed. The medicines I was given didn't work and I coughed all night, every night. When I caught colds, it was even worse; it was downright dangerous as I struggled to breathe. My parents, not really understanding the severity, never took me to the hospital.

By bedtime, I was wheezing badly. I remember being so upset because I didn't want my Christmas ruined. Even more upsetting, I didn't want to ruin anyone else's Christmas. My sister and I put on the new nightgowns our mother bought for us and said our goodnights. My dad and stepmother took turns checking on me. Even the cat, who I had rescued the previous summer by leaving a trail of bologna to entice her out from under a bush, came to sit with me. It was clear to me that she was worried as well. Her presence comforted me.

At some point during the night, everyone went to bed. My sister slept soundly in the twin bed next to me while I heard my dad snoring in the next room. Wide awake and struggling to get air into my lungs, I wanted to go into my dad's room and have him call 9-1-1, but I didn't have the energy to get up. I thought about yelling for him, but I couldn't. Suddenly, an icy feeling of dread crept up my spine. For the first time ever, I had a very real fear that I was going to die. I was going to die on Christmas.

Starting to feel faint, I knew this was the end. As I felt a feeling of letting go, I heard a woman's voice in the direction of the bedroom door. Looking up, I saw a small figure glowing in the space between the door molding and the ceiling, about six or seven inches high. She looked familiar, but I didn't know why. She was wearing a light blue robe and what looked like a white scarf, draped over her head. I couldn't see the details of her face, but I saw her long brown hair.

She was talking but I wasn't catching what she was saying. I was afraid at first. Was I dreaming? Then I heard very clearly, *Carol, you will be alright. It's not your time. I'm watching over you.*

Her words wrapped around me like a warm blanket, and I felt my breathing start to improve. Squinting to get a better look at her, I recognized her. It was Mother Mary. Or at least, she looked like all the images of Mother Mary I had seen throughout my young life. Frozen in my bed, I watched her image slowly dissolve, the way it does in the movies, her words still with me. The room was dark again. My sister was still sound asleep. A little while later, I fell asleep myself.

In the morning, my dad came to check on me. I was still not breathing well, but it was about 50 percent better than it had been during the night. My fear of dying was gone. I didn't tell anyone what happened because I didn't think they'd believe me. I wasn't even sure what I had experienced was real, but the words Mother Mary spoke stayed with me and it's the greatest gift I've ever received.

Carol Campos

MY PATH

*H*aving woken up with a dull throbbing in the front of my head, I was oblivious to the importance of my pain, but I wouldn't let it stand between me and my coaching session. I'd much rather sit with Sylvia, exploring in agony than wait out the end of it in the muffled darkness of my bedroom.

"Why didn't you call in sick? We could have moved it to next week," she said, not understanding the urgency I felt.

She was right though; it wasn't a wise decision to drive my car in this condition and have a conversation on top of it. However, I arrived, ready to dive deeper into my own purpose.

Sylvia had a fitting idea for the moment. I would sit with my eyes closed and without having to say or think much, I would use my imagination while she guided me on a hike through a forest of my liking.

Fine, I thought.

Sitting in a faded red cubic chair, I glanced out the windows. There were hardly any distractions in front of me—just a couple of empty parking spots, a fence, and some sunlit, tall trees.

When I was comfortable, Sylvia started a staccato of questions. "What does your forest look like?"

I didn't see anything with my eyes closed, so I made something up. The forest was an easy pick. Close by the ocean, I remembered the moss-covered dunes with many shrubberies and low oaks with their low hanging branches. Occasionally, you would have to duck to pass underneath, even when walking on the winding sand paths. I loved the lightness of this forest thanks to the many openings in the canopy.

"What season is it?" she asked.

Before closing my eyes, I had seen the fresh green leaves outside the windows, so it seemed only logical to say spring.

"How about sounds. What do you hear?"

I heard the birds chirping outside, so I went with that. Sylvia asked me to repeat my answers and speak up a bit as I was mumbling softly. The talking hurt my head. Feeling like I was easing into a dream, my imagination began taking over. An awareness within grew and I was actually seeing things. I suddenly realized that I was wearing a tidy gray suit and freshly ironed white shirt. I saw rain puddles on the pathway reflecting the trees and white clouds surrounded by the impeccable bright blue sky.

"Do you enjoy walking there?"

"Actually, I am not really walking."

I didn't feel the ground beneath my feet. It felt more like floating while following the trail. She asked me to get my feet on the ground. It took quite some effort as the broken shells that covered the path made a cracking sound under the leather soles of my dress shoes. Needing to get rid of my tidiness, I stamped in the puddles and felt the sandy water splash my pants. I felt a sense of relief and walked on.

"What else do you see?"

Out of nowhere, a fork in the road appeared in front of me. To the right, my romantic forest continued, but the left showed a different scene. The straight trees stood tall, and where the branches and leaves met high up, there was hardly any room for the sunlight. In the gloomy darkness, I saw a straight black asphalted path. The dampness made it feel muggy. Without hesitation, I turned left.

My eyes started to adjust to the dimly lit nature. Besides the sound of my shoes on the well-maintained road, there was silence. I was well out of place in my inappropriate clothing style, but it didn't bother me.

After a short walk, there was a big tree trunk across the path in front of me. I wondered if I was unwanted. I didn't care. Nothing would stop me now. Gripping the rough tree bark with my fingers, I climbed over and kept walking on the path.

Someone asked me, *Is this where you are meant to be?*

Sylvia had faded to the background of my awareness.

No! I shouted.

Immediately I turned right, off the path, pushing the waist high twigs and leaves aside. Zigzagging between the trees to find my way, I saw sunlight in the distance. As I headed towards it, I saw an opening in the canopy. The opening revealed a perfectly round meadow with high grasses and some small, colored flowers, their fragrance filling the air. Moving closer, I saw a man-made barrier around it. Dozens of straight tree trunks lined the outer edge of the meadow. In the distance, I heard the crashing waves on the beach. The ocean was nearby.

I sensed someone; I was not alone. A deer stood proudly in the center of the meadow and looked straight at me. I felt my knees weaken. The animal had majestic antlers with a white glow in the center. In that bright glow, I saw a symbol emerge which I couldn't fully see.

As I intended to move forward, I realized there were two people standing to the right of the deer. I knew them well. My grandfather looked at me with a loving smile. I felt so welcome by his presence as he was the person who introduced me to yoga and Spirit in different, subtle ways. Clearly, our connection was still strong after his passing.

The other person was Lucia. I had only spoken with her once, however, it had been an intense conversation in which she spoke about a magical world unseen to me. It had all felt incredibly powerful and real, and now she seemed to want to prove to me its reality. But above all, she wanted to support me.

They both welcomed me in this peaceful meadow to show me my guide. The deer seemed to be some sort of spirit guide, but I realized he was more than that. He was my future self, a consciousness I would become when ready.

Suddenly, the tables turned, and there were many people in the forest looking at me secretly, hiding in the dark behind the trees. Their auras lit up like the full moon in a clear sky. Many of them were people whom I loved dearly. Still, it made no sense why they were all staring at me. Why weren't they here with me in the meadow?

As I thought it, they instantly joined me. I felt our intense loving connection as we all held hands and an energy lit up around what now turned out to be not one, but two deer. Standing in a large circle, a blue and yellow light swirled around everyone. We floated upward, spiraling with the energy around the two deer, connected with each other and all that was around us.

"Are you where you are supposed to be?"

With great calmness and conviction, I answered, "Yes, I am."

Jeroen van Wieren

MY NIGHT WITH JESUS

woke up at 4:00 o'clock in the morning, wide awake, reminded of a difficult situation with a family member I hadn't seen in a very long time. Grieving, I knew I needed to stop radiating sadness and feel the wonderful memories instead. Closing my eyes, I began remembering all the good times. Connecting to the person, I saw them in a room, and I felt far away from myself. It was like being in two places at the same time. Shining a light, I focused on the fun times. Although I saw a lot of darkness, sadness, and trauma, I kept shining.

Two angels appeared—one on each side of me. Cupping their bright wings, we shined our lights together. Blown away by what was happening, I almost jumped back in shock, but I remembered my spiritual teacher told me it was important to trust and lean in. As I did, the love and kindness of the angels was humbling and filled me with gratitude. A bright figure appeared; I knew it was Jesus. Taking my place in the middle, he stood slightly more forward than the angels.

As I felt myself returning to my body, I thought, *Wait, what about what we were doing?*

Jesus and the angels continued shining their lights. *There are some things only I can do,* he said.

I returned to my body, and abruptly flew straight up. It felt like I was in two places at once, but I could feel my body less and less. Without pain, worries, heaviness, and sadness, I wondered if I was dying. Sensing this was out of my control, I decided to trust and let go.

Do you know that I'm your friend? I asked.

I saw an image of holding hands, which meant yes.

Are you disappointed in me?

I received an emphatic, *No.*

I cried.

Encircled by fluffy pink, blue, and yellow cloud-like surroundings, I became part of a massive being, as if a quilt covered the entire planet and my patch was seamlessly woven into it. I recognized myself in this blanket, and at the same time, I felt completely connected to everyone and everything. I was amazed by how peaceful, light, and worry-free I felt.

Moving up further, I saw three blindingly bright lights surrounded by more fluffiness. Jesus showed me my family and included another child. My husband and I had been trying to have another baby for a year without results. Having accepted this, I felt completely at peace with either outcome. Jesus told me this new child would be energetically like me and showed the child right beside me in our family line. I had no doubt this child was coming.

Will my husband believe me? I asked.

Yes, but he can't have this same experience.

I have been angry with people at times, including you. I have failed, I said.

It was dismissed and wiped away. *It is understood you will have feelings. Do not stay in a state of anger. Connect to me, and act with this feeling as much as you can. Be in this state as much as possible. You will be human. That is okay. You are loved as you are. Show this love to others as much as you can. Honor me by honoring others.*

Slammed back into my body, I felt a lot of uncomfortable energy, heat in my uterus, and sensed a reassuring message of *Let me work.* I knew the physical sensation was a healing one, so I stayed with it as energy moved around my uterus, intestines, and kidneys.

After some movement in these lower organs, it shot up to my heart. I saw my heart with this bright light inside and three huge cracks where the light escaped, showing me where my heart had broken. The light sealed those three places, leaving only a trace of the cracks behind. What was once broken open was now just lines where these injuries had existed.

The energy went back down to my uterus, intestines, and kidneys, and I thought, *This is kind of painful.* I was shown the crucifixion. *Fair enough,* I thought, *I'm shutting up now. Sorry about that.*

After a lengthy time of hot and painful energy in my uterus, it moved all the way up my body, past my throat to my eustachian tubes, and then into my head. It was like a sparkler firework spinning in my head.

Waking up feeling rested, I told my husband about my experience, and he did believe me. I did not include the part about the baby at this time.

Early the next morning, I heard a voice say, *Now. It's time.* I knew what it meant. I woke my husband up and knew we were making a baby. Two weeks later, I was pregnant, and my husband was shocked.

The baby is everything Jesus said he would be—sweet, kind, loving, and a wonderful little friend and helper. Any time I told this story or mentioned Jesus while I was pregnant, my baby would jump and flip and roll—just one more confirmation of the experience I had with Jesus that night.

Lara Jaeger

THE ANOINTED ONE

Upon awakening, I felt an urge to visit a big Mind Body Spirit show in Westminster, London. Previously, I had no desire to visit, as the show had become commercial, and I was already familiar with the work of most of the exhibitors. So, I was a little irritated, as it meant an expedition by train into London followed by a long wait in the queue for entry and a day of mingling with crowds of people. Not exactly my idea of fun. However, I decided to follow my instinct anyway, and by late morning, I was walking around the large exhibition hall.

I recalled the first time I had ever been to this annual exhibition. Back then, it had been an amazing catalyst for self-discovery as I moved from stall to stall, learning about natural therapies, various spiritual paths, healing, crystals, kirlian photography, and all manner of psychic phenomena. Certainly, it had been a lot of fun then.

Now though, it seemed pointless to cover old tracks, and I soon left the razzmatazz and frenzy of the place. Heaving a huge sigh of relief, I made my way back towards the tube station. My footsteps took me past the glorious Roman Catholic Westminster Cathedral, built in the neo-Byzantine style, with striking, intricate brickwork, which dominates the piazza. My intention was to meditate there for a little while, bathing in its peaceful stillness before returning home.

Emerging from the side streets, my consciousness became very expanded. I stopped on the edge of the piazza. As I took in the panoramic scene before me, I noticed a figure of a young man with shoulder length hair and beard. He was in his twenties, of Middle Eastern appearance, and dressed in simple white clothes. He sat quietly on the front steps of the Cathedral entrance, with a simple wooden staff beside him.

My heart skipped a beat and started to fill with bliss. *What was he doing?* I could see and feel that he held the whole area in his heart. In fact, the whole area seemed to be an extension of his heart, and he appeared to be pouring his love out into it. I was included in that outpouring of grace. I continued walking slowly towards him, as if in a waking dream. My awareness held in my heart, expanding with bliss and gratitude for the immensity of the blessing. I was indeed in the presence of a very great being.

In awe, I did not dare break the silence as I walked past him, still sitting on the step, still offering his silent blessing out onto the people in the piazza. I dove into the darkness of the pews and sat, stunned to savor this auspicious darshan in the peace and silence of the cathedral. I prayed for my loved ones and sent up my prayer for all who were in need.

When I eventually emerged from the cathedral, he was gone. Renewed in Spirit, l carried the blessing in my heart. That evening, as I watched the news report on television, I discovered that earlier in the day, there had been extensive riots in London, very close to where I had visited, but they had been successfully contained. The blessing in my heart was a reminder that Grace moves in mysterious ways.

Sw. Prakashananda Saraswati

REST IN THIS

est in this, a commanding yet gentle voice said.

Wait, whose voice was that? Making sure I was fully awake from my Saturday afternoon nap, I listened intently as I felt a sensation of being swaddled like a baby by giant angel wings in a huge hug. Instantly feeling comforted, I allowed my body to sink into the warmth of the hug while the voice continued.

Rest in this. All is well. All is as it should be. You have saved this one and many others. Let them take over. You have done your part. It is time for you to rest. Rest in this. You are exactly where you are meant to be. I will take care of you and have sent others to do so. This man will do so. The friends I have sent you will do so. Rest in this.

Running a domestic violence shelter on the overnight shift for six years had taken a toll on me. The vicarious trauma from listening to and seeing the resulting injuries from the worst and most dangerous night of another human being's life is devastating, especially for an empath.

While being the sole caregiver to my 90-year-old mother was a beautiful privilege, it was also tiring and stressful. Since my beloved mother was aging and requiring more attention, I moved in with her so she could continue living safely in her own home. Her well-being came before my sleep during the daytime hours and so driving to doctor visits, the beauty shop, grocery store, vet appointments, and other errands were added to my daily activities. Her two diabetic dogs needed shots twice daily, and since she was unable to do them, they too became part of my routine.

Exhaustion became the norm. At ten o'clock every night, I tucked Mom into bed and left for work. On my way home from work in the mornings, I often stopped in a parking lot to get a ten-minute nap in my car just to drive the rest of the way home without falling asleep at the wheel.

Feeling like I could no longer go on this way, I prayed for guidance and direction. Would I be able to leave my overnight job to spend more time with my mom? I felt it was the right thing to do, but there were those nagging questions. *Was I doing the right thing? How would I get by without the paycheck?*

But on that Saturday afternoon, upon waking from a nap, the voice found me.

Rest in this.

Immediately, there was a "knowing" that filled my heart and mind with indescribable peace. These were phrases I would have never used, so I knew it didn't come from my own imagination. Just as the words, *You have saved this one and many others* were spoken, Kit, a six-week-old kitten I rescued from a home with domestic violence, walked past my ear and purred, as if confirming those words. The voice also said, *I will take care of you and have sent others to do so. This man will do so.* I later realized the voice was referring to my boyfriend who had been napping with me.

This experience gave me the confidence I needed to leave the shelter and spend more time with Mom. For the next month, Mom and I enjoyed going out for lunches and beginning projects she wanted done to her home. Because of the voice and my trust in it, my mom and I spent the most beautiful last month of her life together making memories I will forever cherish.

Debi Menzer

ROSE

ivine light doesn't always show in the way you expect. There's a fear that can come from experiencing the unfamiliarity of the other side.

As a child, I had experiences where I felt the presence of beings. Before age four, I had two souls that accompanied me. The first one I could see. She was older with dark skin and a scarf on her head. With a God-loving energy, I knew she was there to look after me. The second was a young girl who played with me. I smile when I think about how it gives a completely different slant to the thought of a child's imaginary friend. As an only child at the time, we played quietly for hours on the soft blue rug in the living room of my family's apartment. I remember a peaceful, quiet play, without disagreements.

As I grew older and more rooted in the physical world, it seemed unnatural to have spirit friends. No one else talked about it and I just stopped seeing them. When we moved from the apartment to a large house, I started to see and sense other beings again. In a new space, adjusting to another lifestyle, I did not welcome them; I found it unsettling.

Years passed and I was in denial and as far away from spirits as possible. Until I met Rose.

Home with my parents on a Saturday, I lay on the couch while they sat engrossed in a spy thriller movie. We said nothing to each other, and I remember the comfort of the company even without interaction. The soft couch lulled me to nap. At the long back end of the coral-colored couch, I drifted off to the relaxing sound of the television.

Roughly 15 minutes later, I was in a semi dream state. Although asleep, I could hear everything around me. Suddenly, I came back to consciousness and felt a force, like something, or more accurately, someone pushing themselves into my body.

I felt myself being lifted, and although my eyes were closed, I sensed myself as high as the ceiling, floating right below the ceiling fan. Someone was there from the other side. I panicked.

Tossing and squirming, I tried to scream but no sound came out, only muffled moans. Now fully awake but not fully in control of my body, it was suddenly gone. I was all mine again, albeit shocked. The time span was probably less than 30 seconds, but it seemed like an hour. Time slowed in the experience, and I remember the fear of something completely unknown presenting itself.

My parents sat unaware and unable to understand. Their movie interrupted, they looked over at me with little interest.

"Something crazy just happened!" I told them. "Someone was trying to get inside my body!"

My parents looked at each other with amusement. "You just had a bad dream," my mom said. "You've always had very real feeling dreams, you're just that way. Forget about it, just relax."

I was mad; I felt they judged my experience. "It wasn't a dream!" I shouted at them.

They shrugged and turned back to their movie. Over the years, they'd probably grown indifferent to my "weird experiences." I got up and stormed out of the room, shaken and furious. It was a frustration I knew well, experiencing things other people hadn't. It felt lonely.

For the first time in years, I thought back to the spirits of my childhood. I didn't sense any evil intention from the spirit. It all happened so fast—like two people accidentally bumping into each other.

I didn't sleep well for a while. As if an invisible line had been drawn, I would look into the living room, but dared not go in. At night, that sentiment was doubled. A big open space, the living room was the heart of the home where family laughed and spent time together with games and TV. I missed being in the room.

A few weeks passed and one afternoon I stopped and looked in. The room looked harmless. Not quite five o'clock, daylight streamed through the three large windows that overlooked the yard. Curiosity quelled fear. I walked in. Nothing. I sat on the couch, near but not in the same spot I'd been lying the last time.

After a few minutes, my confidence grew and I grabbed the remote, turning on the television. The history channel appeared on the screen, telling a story about a child whose parents were concerned when she told them of a man she played with in the backyard. The child described the man's appearance in great detail, but the parents saw no one. After some research, they found out that the man who fit the description was deceased and had once owned the home. Chills buzzed through my body. I knew the story on television was not a coincidence.

I wasn't afraid, in fact, I felt protected. As I felt a gentle caress on my cheek, I heard a message in my head that said, *What happened was an accident. I'd never hurt you.*

Instantly, I knew her name was Rose and that she'd had a family in this house, on this property, or nearby. I understood she was looking out for me and what I had experienced on the couch had been unintentional. I'm not sure she understood it herself.

The house and property looked different as I reflected on spans of time and lives that had been there. It seemed we didn't own it but shared it with all the different lives throughout time. There was a giant tree across the way, and in my mind, I imagined Rose sitting there or on a swing.

I knew the moment I went back in the room and picked up the remote that the story of the spirit was waiting for me. A Divine message. The child had seen the man in the yard, and they were connected. I thought back to when I was a child and didn't question such happenings. They felt as natural as breathing or playing with my toys. I knew Rose was connected to me because she sensed that openness, that portal. I was born open to these connections—a gift to help other people. I stopped fearing the other side and was ready to explore.

A few months later, I visited a psychic. After traveling a couple of hours because she was supposed to be that good, I sat down, and she began scribbling as it helped her "see." She gave me some details she could not have known about my life, and I was impressed. About a third of the way into the session, she stopped scribbling, looked up, and asked, "Who's Rose?"

I decided not to share the details and said I wasn't sure. I wanted to know what she knew.

"Rose is all around you," she said, "She protects you."

When I would return to the living room, I would feel her. I'd feel a little chill or tingle and I'd look up and ask, "Rose?"

Some people believe when you are contacted by spirits it's because they need or want something from you, but I knew Rose didn't want anything. She was at peace. All she wanted was for me to know that things would be okay and that there are souls on the other side that watch out for us.

Her Divine presence was part of the beginning experiences that guided me towards my work. When she made herself known to me it was to show me that there is love and beauty in the supernatural; nothing to be feared. Her light evidenced to me the light we all have, a light that continues past this world. Our job is to nurture our light and help others with theirs. I thank Rose for teaching this.

Jennifer Herrera

EVERYTHING IS ALL RIGHT

"Chhhh, chhhh, chhhh." I could hear the blood oozing out of my body with each beat of my heart, like water gushing out of a faucet.

"Lord Jesus! Lord Jesus!" a desperate voice cried out.

The voice belonged to one of the nuns at the Catholic hospital where I had just given birth to my third son. It had been a hard labor of hours of clenching back pain with no contractions before I could push the baby out.

After the birth, I drifted away.

"You have a boy!" I heard the doctor say, trying to get my attention.

I said nothing.

Then again, "You hear me, you have another boy!"

I could barely manage a "hmmm" in response. I was so happy my labor was over and that the baby was safe.

Some time later, a sudden noise and commotion jarred me out of my sleep. I sensed panic and alarm as I was being pushed at top speed on a gurney to the operating room. We were going so fast that we kept bumping into things. *What's happening?*

I had started hemorrhaging profusely. The medical team of three doctors and nurses worked frantically to stop the bleeding. I was fading in and out but could hear the desperation and panic in the doctors' voices. They started to massage my abdomen to try to stop the bleeding. With each massage, I could hear the blood continue oozing out of my body. It sounded like someone had turned a tap on and left it running.

Feeling the blood pulse out of me, I knew. *Oh my God, I am dying.* All I could see were the little faces of my three and six year old sons. They were so happy that mommy was going to the hospital to have their baby brother or sister and now I was abandoning them. I thought of my husband. My heart was aching and breaking that I would never see them again. *I won't be going home. We will never see each other again.*

I cried out, "Not yet, God, not yet! Now is not the right time. I want to be with them, to raise them, to be their mother and teacher."

I grew colder and colder as the blood left my body. I was desperately clinging to life. Who can I turn to for help?

"Oh, please help me, dear Jesus."

A sense of peace washed over me with a deep inner knowing that God was the only one that could help me pull through this critical time. Breathing a deep sigh of relief, I surrendered my life to God, knowing that all would be okay. I wasn't afraid anymore. I was no longer bargaining.

Lying there in the hospital, my body growing more and more like a block of ice, I began reciting the 23rd Psalm in my mind as I had as a child and throughout my life when I faced difficulty. *The Lord is my shepherd, I shall not want, he maketh me to lie down in green pastures...*

Halfway through the prayer, I left my body and the room and arrived someplace else. I woke up lying in a green pasture, vast beautiful, lush green fields rolling out in all directions in my peripheral view. As I became more aware, I found myself sitting on a rock where a powerful being, surrounded by glowing blue light, was gently and lovingly stroking the left side of my head. *Everything is all right. Everything is all right. Everything is all right.*

I knew in my heart this energy was the Jesus I had loved my whole life. Feeling bathed in unconditional love and golden light, it reminded me of being a child and the times I had called out in prayer to God. Every cell of my being was bathed in happiness that Jesus was there with me. I accepted without question what he was saying, *Everything is all right now.*

I had no sense of my body or of time passing. I was in pure communion with Spirit, with Jesus, in the land of pure potential where God lives. Letting go of all the things that had seemed so important, I rested in that Presence. Then there was silence.

Some time later, I heard a voice in the distance softly calling my name. It was my doctor's voice calling me. I slowly came back to my body. Opening my eyes, I realized that to everyone else, I was already dead. The light in the room was dim, the doctors and nurses had stopped working on me, and I was covered up to my neck with a white sheet. A priest was beside me giving me the last rites of the church. The nurses and my doctor stood shoulder to shoulder against the wall, tears streaming down their cheeks.

My doctor walked up to me, and I could see the disbelief in his eyes that I had returned. He said I had gotten so low on blood that they had to call in the priest. Even then I could see the doctor wasn't sure I was going to make it. He asked the priest to continue with the prayers. The priest was still beside me, white as a sheet. I am not sure he had ever seen so much blood before in his life.

I was feeling so weak and tired that I could hardly speak or keep my eyes open. While the priest was saying the prayers, I was silently saying my own, *Thank the Lord and praise the Lord* repeatedly until I drifted off to a peaceful, restful sleep.

It was touch and go for two weeks before I was finally allowed to go home to my dear little boys, with my newborn son. I took with me the knowing that

God is always here for me, and I am always loved. When I was with Jesus, he used the present tense in his reassurance. He didn't say, *everything is going to be all right.* He said, *everything is all right.* And now I walk in the world with that thought, *everything is all right.*

Maylin Lue Pann

GUARDIAN ANGEL

I don't remember my grandad; he died when I was two years old, so I have only seen pictures of him. Known for his roll-up cigarettes and a navy trench coat he practically lived in, I was told he adored me and would do anything for me.

An only child, my parents were much older than most of my friends' parents. My mum nearly 40, and my dad 55, had numerous health issues which prevented them from strenuous activity and made them appear older. Consequently, I was often left to entertain myself.

When I was five years old, I was excited about our annual family holiday. Since neither of my parents drove, we had to take a taxi to the coach stop and then travel five hours on the coach to the seaside town of Great Yarmouth.

We had a lovely time so far, visiting the amusement arcades, having ice creams and cockles, and enjoying the freedom of being beside the sea instead of at home in the East End of London. One warm, sunny day, we decided to spend the day at the beach. Since none of us could swim, my parents chose to sit on deck chairs at the back of the beach, far away from the sea. I played on the golden sand for hours, making sandcastles with my bucket and spade, my mum helping me go down to the sea and fill my bucket with water to make the sand supple so my castles stood tall and proud. When I asked my parents if we could go down to the sea one more time to collect more water, my mum was tired and didn't want to come. She said I could go by myself as long as I was careful.

Once down by the water, I was mesmerized by the waves rolling in and crashing on the beach. Watching people swimming, relaxing, splashing, and having fun in the water, I decided to put my toes in. The water was warmer than I imagined and tickled my toes causing me to laugh out loud as I ran gingerly between the beach and the water.

I turned to see a man watching me. He asked if I was having fun, and I said I was. He asked if I was willing to be a bit braver and whether I had "boinged" in the sea before. I told him I hadn't as I couldn't swim. He told me I didn't need to be able to swim, just jump. I thought, *That sounds easy, I can do that*, so I started jumping over the waves as they came in. He was right; this was fun. Until I got too confident and didn't realize how much further I had gone out.

The next wave was much bigger, and I lost my footing and went under. I could feel myself rolling around in the wave, water going up my nose and seaweed wrapping itself around my body and face. Panicking, I felt myself being yanked out of the water by my bathing suit. As I gathered my bearings, thankful to be back on the sand again, I turned to thank my rescuer. It was the man who had shown me how to boing.

Heading back to the safety of my parents, I was about to ask the man to come with me, but he was gone. When I told my parents what had occurred, they were horrified at what could have happened. We looked for the man to thank him, but he was nowhere to be found.

Many years later, while walking on the beach with the water rolling over my feet, I was doing some soul searching and talking to Spirit. That memory came back to me as clear as day, and for the first time, I remembered that the man standing with me, the one that yanked me out of the water, had been wearing that same blue trench coat.

Anita Weeks

UNSEEN AND CONNECTED

$\mathcal{Y}$ears ago, before the advent of the cell phone, my husband was posted on a new assignment in an unfamiliar city. We had moved into a one-story house with a long driveway lined with coconut trees and a canal running behind the house. I had noticed two children in the house opposite ours, but we had not met as a family. Busy with school admissions and setting up our new home, we had no time for socializing, and I had not established any contacts in the city.

Soon after our arrival, my husband had to fly to another city for work. In the afternoon, our six-year-old started a fever, and soon after my husband left, his temperature started rising. By late evening, his fever was raging, and I was alone with him and my four-year-old.

Paracetamols acted as a temporary palliative. I washed his head at regular intervals to keep the temperature down. As the evening progressed into night, the three of us sat together, giving each other courage and comfort. The darkness and silence of the black outside made us feel even more isolated from the world. The moon seemed to have gone into hibernation too.

The living room led into a small covered sitting space with large glass windows. A couple of chairs and the phone, placed on a stool, occupied the space. Suddenly, the deafening stillness was sharply slashed by the ringing of the phone. Jolted out of the chair, I ran to answer it, sure it was my husband calling.

An unknown but well-modulated voice, speaking good English, was on the other end. "Good evening. Am I speaking to Mrs. Banerjea?" he asked.

"Yes," I replied, hesitantly.

"Ma'am your husband left for the airport this evening?" he asked.

Once again, I replied in the affirmative, wondering why he was confirming with me if he already knew.

"I have called to tell you that there has been an accident and I need you to come to the police station. A person will be coming to pick you up."

I sat quietly for a moment before answering, "Why don't you call the office? If you have this number, you should be able to get the office too. They will know what to do."

This was obviously not the expected response. He seemed to be at a loss for words. I hung up the phone. *What have I done? How is he? I didn't even ask. I need to be at the police station now. How could I give this answer? There has been an accident and I asked him to talk to the office staff. What a ridiculous thing to do.* Thoughts tore through me as I struggled with my action or rather inaction. I could not even call back. *What was I supposed to do?*

My son's temperature had gone up. I had a child who was ill and a confused four-year-old, both of whom needed my immediate attention. There was no time to think. I struggled inside, waiting for dawn to break. Somehow sunlight brought hope with it.

The effect of the medicine and head washing made his temperature recede. I waited for the first sliver of sunlight and the three of us walked across to the house opposite ours. Ringing the bell, I woke them up, telling them I needed their help with a doctor.

As we sat in the car on the way to the hospital, I asked them the whereabouts of the police station. Obviously, they were intrigued with this inquiry, and I recounted to them what had happened, feeling conscience-stricken about what I had done.

"Did the person say he would take you to the police station?"

"Yes, as a matter of fact he did," I answered.

"You have been saved. There is a gang operating in the area. They must have been keeping watch over your house since you are new to the neighborhood, and they knew that you were alone with the children. They have informants who told them that your husband had gone out of station. The natural response would have been to immediately open the door to whoever came to pick you up and then…"

I did not even want to think about what could have happened. The enormity of the situation gradually sank in. After consulting the doctor and checking with the office, I learned that my husband was fine. Relief washed over me with the physical time and mental space to mull over the incident.

Who had spoken through me? It was certainly not a normal response. If anything, it was quite the opposite. And yet the words had spontaneously spilled out. Unseen but deeply felt, the voice was mine, but it was not me. While I was oblivious to the danger lurking so close, it had chosen to manifest itself through my voice and words because that was needed. Since then, I have learned to have faith and believe in the Spirit of the Universe.

Sumita Banerjea

SEVILLE

Sitting with my coffee at a loud and crowded Starbucks in West Los Angeles, I wrote in my leather-bound journal with a heavy heart. My morning started out like every other day in recent weeks—my chaotic mind spiraling with disempowering thoughts as I replayed my dreadful troubles. Sadness, confusion, and resentment poured onto the page. Despite having all kinds of metaphysical and practical tools in hand, I could not circumvent my foul mood let alone solve what seemed insurmountable. My faith in the Divine wavered for the first time since my arrogant psyche could not secure the expected guidance, support, or inspiration. The more I wrote, the more furious I became—to the point where I couldn't keep my enraged body from shuddering. Quickly downing my lukewarm coffee, I packed my stuff into my backpack and stormed out.

Heading down a narrow alleyway, I escaped the busyness of the LA traffic in front of me. With my headphones in, I set out for the nearby park to find some relief. The tension somewhat softened in my mind as the song "Magnificent" by U2 played loudly between my ears.

As I approached the Bad News Bears Park, I noticed an older man sitting on the grass waving at me. I peered behind me to see if he was trying to draw someone else's attention, but no one else was there. Drawing closer to him, I saw signs of his homelessness. The man with disheveled brown-gray hair sat with tattered clothes and an unclean, sun-damaged face. Two soiled bags laid next to him.

"Son! Son! Son!" he exclaimed as he continuously waved his arms to interrupt my hurried stride.

I thought of snubbing his call, but I felt obligated to take off my earphones for this lonesome stranger. There was something familiar about him that stopped me in my tracks.

"May I help you?" I nervously replied as I started to reach into my pocket for some change. I thought to myself, *Here it goes, he wants some money. What else could he want from me?* In most circumstances, I would either lay a dollar bill into an outstretched hand or walk away with a token nod.

The lanky gentleman quickly responded, "Son, will you come sit with me? Don't worry, I don't want anything from you. Just your good ole' company for a moment."

Oddly, I didn't feel alarmed by his strange request. His tranquil vibe and his warm crystal blue eyes made me feel safe in front of the bustling street as pedestrians and cars zoomed by. I dropped my heavy backpack and planted myself on the yellow-green grass.

His calm voice intensified to sheer joy as we exchanged names. He shared delightfully, "Nice to meet you, Sujon. My daddy had me in the back of his caddy, so he nicknamed me Seville. He's in heaven now. I really miss him."

I coyly replied, "I'm sorry to hear that. Nice to meet you, Seville."

"Well, Sir John, I noticed you as you were crossing the street. What a big heart. Your heart is actually bigger than your body, did you know that? The only problem is that it's so blue," he remarked. "I wish I had a golden heart as big as yours."

My guard immediately went up questioning Seville's real intent. His overt compliments were grand, but I was baffled by his comments. How would this vagabond know anything about my heart? My common logic assessed him by his outer appearance as a homeless man down on his luck. I was being a skeptic at best at this point, waiting for his ulterior motive to be revealed.

"What do you mean by that, sir?" I asked him politely.

"Well, son, I could see your heart miles away. Radical. I feel your heart's intensity while you sit here next to me. Are you ready to share it?" he spoke steadfastly as he scrutinized my face. Before I could answer, he continued, "I know you are going through a very hard time, but do you think it can really get any harder than my life?"

Dumbfounded by his accurate assessment, I sat there somewhat tongue-tied struggling to respond. He continued to share, "You are a light being, so go share yourself already. Stop hiding behind all your pain. It's time for you to expose that beautiful heart, especially with your family, friends, and your lover. They need you now more than ever. The world needs you now. Lead the way. Remember, you said you would. It's your choice to make and no one is stopping you but you."

I turned my head towards Seville to size up his face as he spoke with incredible candor much like a shaman elder. I questioned if he was some psychic or clairvoyant who was showing off. Every provocative sentence felt like a punch pummeling me with insights without any underhanded pretense. In this very moment, his mind-blowing assessment seemed to be the perfect balm for my melancholy.

Our offbeat chat continued as we delved into each other's stories. The longer we spoke, the more comfortable I became. Seville was one of the most authentic human beings I had ever met. With his agape love, he openly expressed his journey to homelessness. Seville succumbed to the American economic bubble burst three years prior, surrendering all his money and possessions. This former USC business grad had lost his once thriving business to greedy financial institutions and partners. He regretfully explained how his wife and kids as well as many friends had abandoned him.

Despite his heart-wrenching loss, he pressed on. Now he felt freer than ever. Seville was not the oft judged or stereotypical "bum" on the streets. He was a spiritual warrior.

Our rap session turned sour at one point when Seville vehemently pushed my buttons. He challenged, "Stop your bitch'n. You are playing a martyr. Your excuses are worthless and you're not aware of your real power. Get to know who you are and your cosmic connection. Reclaim the true you."

Triggered by his honest and curt evaluation, fireworks exploded internally. He hit a button in me that couldn't be reversed. Angrily, I defended my position, "Seville you have no idea who I am or what I have been through. I courageously meet all my challenges. I help others with their challenging journeys. I am a seasoned life coach and healer. I know I can pull myself out of this mood at any time. Besides, I am related to a famous Swami, Paramahansa Yogananda. He brought yoga and meditation to the West in 1920. He guides me all the time. So do the rest of my spiritual team."

"Oh, passion and fire – this is the perfect element of alchemy," Seville responded.

Still under a raging storm, I ignored his comment. I proudly pulled Yogananda's picture from my wallet and imperiously displayed it to Seville. He smirked and examined the photo and my face back and forth keenly.

"Wow, you have his eyes. I can see the resemblance in your heart too," he remarked.

Refraining from my arrogant fury, I remained quiet and took some deep breaths. An awkward silence filled the air for a few moments while we gazed onto Ohio Avenue, watching aimlessly as cars passed by.

As the temperature of our discussion simmered, Seville solemnly shared, "It's these times of failure when it's best to plant your seeds of success. Keep your focus on where you are headed and trust that the Divine will nurture you and water your seeds."

Though I couldn't place it, his wisdom-filled words seemed quite familiar. Deep down, I knew he was right. I recognized that he was humbly trying to shift my mood, circumstances, and perhaps even my life–as a selfless offering.

Our peculiar conversation lasted for over an hour. I had even pulled out my journal a few times to write some significant reminders. Entering the portal of Seville was whimsical, fun, intense, and compelling all at the same time as I rode the roller coaster of varied emotions. Seville's quirkiness and fearless personality was infectious. Moments when he spoke, I felt like a child being taught by an authority figure. On several occasions, I witnessed his youthful and juvenile nature come to life as he pranced and danced in the park without any shame or apology. Though at first, I felt uneasy and awkward, I appreciated his sense of freedom and joy. Seville helped me realize that life is to be met with awe and wonder. Meeting Seville brought about incredible appreciation, self-awareness, and light heartedness. Gratitude filled my being as I witnessed this human angel.

The intense vibe finally broke when the theme from Superman rang on my cell phone. Quickly, I silenced the loud ring to prevent an interruption to our flow.

Seville piped up, "How appropriate, the Superman theme. Do you have a red cape underneath, Clark? I mean, you are wearing a Superman ring too," Seville pointed to my finger as he laughed.

I sarcastically jested, "No, I am Super Sujon." I hurriedly placed my pen and journal into my backpack signaling my exit.

Seville broke my wonderment and said, "Well Son, it looks like you are ready to go. What a pleasure to hang, man. You have given me such a gift by putting up with me today."

"Seville, I am the one who feels fortunate. You have given me the gift of a lifetime," I humbly replied as I stood up.

Seville quickly grabbed my leg to interrupt the farewell. "Superman, wait, I have one more thing."

The five foot nine Seville pulled out his frayed wallet from his soiled jeans. Slowly, he opened it up, tugging on something. I presumed he was going to show me a picture of his family because he referenced them often in our conversation. After a few seconds of struggle, he finally pulled out a picture, and turned it toward my face. Stunned, I dropped my backpack and grabbed the photo out of his pinched fingers. An intense wave of emotion ran through my body as I dropped onto the grassy ground. Tears trickled down my cheeks. I was holding the same image of Paramahansa Yogananda that I had shown him much earlier. Seville had never exposed his copy even after I had shared my relationship with Yogananda several times.

"Seville, how can this be?" I shouted. I shook my head continuously in disbelief as I stuttered. "What's this… How… who are you?"

Seville put his hand on my shoulder, crouching down next to me. His powerful eyes transformed into a deep gray-green color as he looked at me. For a moment, he felt and sounded different.

"I know, Son. I know," he calmly said.

It took a couple of minutes to compose myself. I blurted, "Seville you don't know what you have done for me today."

Seville simply winked. "Son, it was all meant to be today. Perhaps Divinely orchestrated," he expressed with authority, pointing to the sky.

I hopped up onto my feet and wiped my tearful face. Pulling out my wallet I retrieved all the cash I had and planted forty-four dollars into his palm. Seville immediately refused. We played reverse tug of war until he finally conceded. My body wobbled while I picked up my belongings and I started to head home. I stopped and asked Seville if I could take a picture of him on my phone.

"No, No, No," he opposed immediately. "I don't look so good. I don't want my family to see me like this."

"It's only for me..." I pleaded. I felt he was quite uncomfortable, so I didn't press him. I waved goodbye and shouted from a distance, "Take care, Seville. Hopefully I will see you again later."

Seville instantly asserted, "It's in God's hands. If he calls, I shall answer. I am sure she will give me another assignment."

That was the first and last time I saw Seville. Although I visited the Bad News Bears Park frequently over the next several weeks, I saw no sign of Seville anywhere.

Sujon Datta

UNFORESEEN SOUL RETRIEVAL

*a*nswering the call from the unseen worlds to go deeper, I lay down one afternoon to journey. As I drifted away, I found myself in an unknown place with a grand, dimly lit room, like a vault in front of me. Someone stood in the corner, and I felt called to move closer. It was my father; he had come forth from the other side for the first time since he passed many years ago.

With his arm raised, he pointed firmly to the right. I tried to connect with his eyes, but the darkness would not allow it. Instead, I turned my head towards the direction of his finger. A faint light glowed, and I moved closer to see a door opening to a small room with three sides, like a portal, for me to enter.

Darkness became light, revealing a young woman on a sarcophagus-like bed. Locked inside this secret crypt, she appeared to be in a deep sleep. Suddenly, I knew who she was—my 16-year-old self. The revelation shook me as I wondered why she was there. *She must come out, I thought. She is not fully alive in here.*

I felt forces around who wanted to burn down the room to let her rest. For a moment, I thought it would be for the best; how else was I to handle her distress and immense and explosive strength. Then an inner voice came in so strong, telling me I could not let that be. Fire can spread uncontrollably, but I was here to set her free, that girl once me. She was ready to come out and ready to come home. I turned my head to look at my father, but he seemed to have backed off into a dark corner.

Looking out to the grand vault, I saw a staircase in obscure light. A woman in white stood at the top, her face not quite visible and her hair in what appeared an old-fashioned style. Her energy filled the whole room. An inscrutable vision, I somehow knew she was the one overseeing everything—a guide making sure I could handle the situation and perhaps the one who sent my father to show me the way. Looking at the outline of her hair and her long, vibrating dress, I could feel her love and fierce determination. All silent but the communication so clear, *Go deep,* she said. *The darkness is not to be feared, it is to be explored. As you enter with an open heart the darkness becomes light and you will open to yourself.* My initial worry vanished, replaced by strength and wisdom. I could handle this with the help of my guide who traveled through all times to greet me in that precious moment.

When I woke up to the world, it felt like I was in a haze, the veil thin and my senses sharpened. As insights unfolded over the next few days, I understood that a new part of my journey had begun. All the right teachers and groups began appearing. I listened to a shaman talk about soul retrievals and I recognized it all from my experience. By setting my 16-year-old self free, I was able to see a new path for me.

Maria Nordin

THE SPIRIT VEILED WOMEN

Sitting in the lobby of the surgical center, I waited with family and friends for the surgeon to tell us the seriousness of my husband's illness. Diagnosed one year prior with a very rare cancer, we knew from the beginning the prognosis was not good. Yet we waited for the surgery to begin, hoping we would receive a more promising outcome.

At this time of my life, I believed in God. I believed in angels. I believed in the connection between heaven and earth. But I never had evidence of this connection or my ability to tap in whenever and wherever for guidance with my life. As I looked around at my family, some had tears in their eyes, some were angry at what we were facing, and some looked as though they were in shock.

Silently I prayed for a different outcome although I knew in my heart this would probably be a stretch. I kept hearing in my mind that no matter the outcome I would be okay, the children would be okay, and that even if he was not here in the physical, our souls would always be connected. This voice scared me. My rational mind could not grasp the true concept of what that meant for me, him, or our children. Together since age 15, we had two beautiful daughters who loved us both very much. Our little unit was such a happy family.

As I sat in the chair with my eyes closed and hands folded deep in prayer, I remembered all that we had been through over the last 25 years. Feeling a tap on my shoulder, I opened my eyes, but no one was there. Within seconds, the doctor walked into the lobby and said, "The family of…"

I never even heard him say my husband's name. I stood up while thinking to myself, *It's only been 30 minutes, he said this would be a four-hour surgery.* He walked over to me and said that my husband was terminal, then he turned around and left the room. My family members were standing around me crying. After only hearing the word "terminal," I heard, *You're all going to be okay.* I kept hearing *This will pass, you will be okay.*

Walking out of the room and down the hallway, I stood waiting by the doors so that I could go in and see him. My family members stayed in the waiting room crying and wailing. Outside the surgery door, I closed my eyes for a brief moment, and when I opened them again, two ladies stood next to me. They were elderly women wearing black clothes with black veils over their heads.

One of them asked me, "Are you a Christian?"

I looked at her and didn't know what to say. In my mind I thought, *I'm Catholic.* But I responded to her by saying "yes."

"I thought so, and you will be fine," she said, "You know what will happen next and you will be fine."

Turning to walk away, I heard my mother's voice behind me as she walked up the hall. I quickly turned back around, and they were gone. The ladies that appeared to let me know that I would be fine…were gone.

A cold sensation ran through my body. My heartbeat slowed and there was a feeling of expansion in my chest. It felt as though my body was calming. In my mind, I felt a sense of clarity. I knew at that moment that I would never be alone. Even if he left this physical world, he would always be with me. It was such a feeling of security. My rational mind couldn't understand why I felt this way. *Why am I okay? Why do I feel safe? And where did they go? Did these women have something to do with why I understood this in a way that no one else did?*

The surgery doors opened, and a nurse said I could come back to the recovery room. As I walked over to my husband, the love of my life, I looked at him with unconditional love.

Opening his eyes, he said, "Babe, am I going to die?"

I paused, taking a deep breath, and said, "I don't really know."

"I think I am. But it will be okay, and I will never really leave you."

When I told him about the veiled women in the hallway he said, "They came to me too and told me that I will come back to you. I will never leave you alone."

Over the next few months, we had many conversations about him coming to visit me when he is physically gone from this place. It's been 20 years since he passed, and he has never really left me.

Jennifer Perez Solar

HEALING GUIDANCE

My nineteen-year-old daughter had experienced an ovarian cyst that left doctors and specialists baffled. They were unsure whether to remove the cyst, if damage to the cyst was preventable, or how much of the ovary she might lose. With so much in question and not hearing the answers we needed to proceed comfortably, I was unsure of what to do. My daughter was in pain and there was a risk of rupture, and I needed to make a decision quickly. Feeling responsible I prayed for her well-being. That night before falling asleep, I asked for guidance.

The next morning, I was fortunate to receive a message from my guide, my twin flame who appears to me in visions. He showed me an etheric picture of a man's tie and pretzels. I became energized and meditated further. I was so intrigued that I physically got a tie and some pretzels to carry around with me all day. I knew by having these shapes and patterns with me, my guide would know I was looking and listening for other clues and deeper meanings. That night, in a dream, my guide appeared and delivered a powerful message.

There he stood, dressed in a magnificently colored cloak, his face filled with light. Shaking a magic wand he demanded, "Tie the Knot!" My body shook and my head went blank.

Tie the knot, I thought. I heard my higher self say in acknowledgement, *Tie the knot, tie the suture.* I knew, in an instant, we were to proceed with the surgery to remove the ovarian cyst.

The surgery was scheduled, and one day later she was in the hospital. An eight-centimeter cyst was successfully removed. She was discharged and sent home to heal and rest.

As the days passed, post-surgery healing was uncomfortable. Medication could not control the pain she was enduring. My daughter was exhausted, pale, and weak. I looked at her, as any mother would, with distress, love, and curiosity. I quietly asked myself what I could do to help. Looking internally intuition began to flow.

I remembered pain as "stuck" energy—energy that is bound-up and devoid of flow and thought, *I need to move this energy.* Somehow, I needed to help her in the spaces where medicine could not reach; I needed to access parts of her body for which there are no names. Flashes of healing devices came to mind—sound bowls, drums, frequency machines, and then I heard a female voice say, *Tuning forks, get them all.*

With her instruction to get the tuning forks, I went to my studio and grabbed all twenty-four of them—twelve or more of which are frequencies of the organs, some are mineral frequencies, and others have tones to help calm the nervous system. I did not know what to expect, but I listened intently and placed all the forks alongside my daughter. As she lay asleep, I stood over her not knowing where to start. I grabbed a fork, and my guide "took" my hands and guided me through a profound healing.

My mind could not keep up. It was fast, unprecedented, and unpredictable. There was no reason for which fork was coming next to synchronize with her aura and sound body to bring equilibrium. She lay there asleep and unaware of this transmission. For me, the notes and tones created a euphoric feeling throughout my body. As time went on, I couldn't feel any sense of belonging with my body. I became total sound and light in space. There was no thought, no worry, no fear, no parenting, no preconceived thought that I had to fix everything.

As the healing continued, my hands grabbed forks and holding them loosely, moved the forks over her body in the most rhythmic way. Turning, twisting, and tuning delicately at every angle, the sounds harmonizing in a way that excited my being.

After a few more minutes all movement, sound, and energy subsided. My body was exhausted from the healing. I could feel my blood pulsing and heart beating as if I had run a mile very quickly. I looked at my daughter. She was still sleeping quietly just as she had been for the last hour. I was tired and unsure what to think or do, so I laid silently on the floor next to her. I chose one tuning fork to use on myself to ground me and return myself to a coherent state.

For about half an hour, I gave myself the space and time to process all that happened. Afterward, I went into the kitchen for some water. In that time, my daughter woke drenched in sweat, completely soaked from the tones and energetics that she had absorbed.

"What happened?" she asked, "I'm soaked."

Still in some shock, I wasn't sure what to say until I heard the words from my guide, *She's been purified.*

"I feel better. The pain is mostly gone," my daughter said.

She was able to sit without pain, walk without pain, eat, and regain complete strength all within three to six hours of the energy exchange. Each moment, she felt recharged and stronger. Each day, she expressed a new level of comfort and experienced more activity. By day four, my daughter was on a plane to Boston for her college orientation and to begin her freshman year.

Tamara Knox

SAL TAUGHT ME TO BELIEVE

When I first started working as a medium, doors of opportunity flew open for me. Invitations for things I'd never done before flooded in. Rational skipped fear and went straight out the window.

"Sure, I can do that platform reading in front of a large group," stumbles out of my mouth about something I have never done before. "Yes, I can do that party."

I sat in a loud, crowded room, delivering information to a row of shocked strangers and shocked myself. "How can you know that?" they would say to me. I would shrug and say, "I don't know," but I was doing it. No experience. Never having done it before.

"Yes" was the only word I would say when asked to do something with my gifts. Something bigger than me had my puppet strings and was directing me about where to go, what to do, and what to say. Although I was still skeptical of my gifts, I possessed a courage I didn't even know I had. Little did I know that the puppet masters and Sal were my guides, and they were bringing me home to my soul.

One day, I receive a call from a woman who asks me to clear a restaurant. I am comfortable reading spaces. Clearing it? Well, I have some ideas, so why not? The puppet master pulls his strings, and I comply.

I arrive at Sunset Boulevard—nervous but with strange confidence creeping in. Hand on the door, I pat my bag of good, old-fashioned energy-clearing paraphernalia—sage, white candle, vodka, lavender oil, bell, and wooden matches because you can't use a lighter. Don't ask me how I know you can't use a lighter; I just know. These are the strange things I know but have never been taught.

Later, I read an energy-clearing book that confirms, "Always use wooden matches." Validations like these help me believe in my gifts. The vodka and lavender part came from my grouchy old tarot teacher, who hated me. Don't ask me how I know she hated me; I just know.

Grabbing the heavy door handle, I step inside. The beautiful restaurant is open and airy, welcoming me inside. I take another step in, and boom, I'm gasping for air. Feverishly, I look for the cause of my sudden lack of breath. I look to the right and see a row of windows facing the famous Sunset Plaza courtyard and to the left and see a brick wall that is tastefully filled with candles. The tables are covered with white cloths and pristine place settings. A piano in the middle of the room holds the promise of a seductive ambiance to dine by. I search for the reason for my lack of breath. Was this fear? I check in with my heart. Nope, not anxious. And then, it hits me. There must be a ghost.

Cautiously, I step further in, looking for some people. From the back of the restaurant, a tall, beautiful, dark-haired woman comes toward me.

"You must be Marilyn," she says, reaching her hand out to shake mine.

"Yes, I am. It's nice to meet you."

She calls out to the restaurant owner to come meet me. Peter, a typical Brooklyn Italian man, approaches me. He represents all the unpleasant experiences with Brooklyn Italian men in my youth—the type my mother, after her own fated experience, told me never to marry. As much as she tried to raise me differently, growing up with three older Italian brothers in a very antiquated culture, I am branded with the knowledge to protect myself from these types of men.

"How you doing?" Peter says in a deep voice with a slight Brooklyn accent.

He sizes me up. I do the same to him. It's obvious we both attended Streetwise Brooklyn 101. I know Peter doesn't trust me or even believe in what I do. It's clear his girlfriend hired me.

I look him in the eye and give him a firm handshake, revealing that I know his neighborhood and have been to the same school and conveying not to mess with me.

The puppet master pulls my strings. Ignoring my hurt history, I walk around the restaurant.

Peter's girlfriend explains that the restaurant has been open for a month and has not been doing as well as they had hoped. Peter's other restaurant, which is on the other side of Sunset Plaza, is super successful, so it makes little sense.

"So, what is it you do?" Peter asks with amusement in his voice.

"I am a medium. I talk to your guides, who are always with you, and I speak to the dead."

I swear I hear a small laugh. Brushing it off, I continue walking around.

With each step I take, my breathing becomes more difficult. Something heavy is hiding in this restaurant. It has to be a ghost. The tools I brought will not do the trick. I consider taking a swig of vodka for confidence but drinking on the job as a medium brings a whole slew of other problems.

The puppet master pulls my strings and brings me back into the present as the connection grows stronger.

As I continue to walk around the brightly lit restaurant, everything looks new, clean, and airy. Still, with all this open air, I can't breathe. *Why the lack of air? There has to be a ghost. Where is it?* I think to myself.

"I can't breathe," I tell them.

I walk over to the wall of white candles and realize they are fake. Peter follows behind me, his skepticism a heavy cloud hanging over us. I point to the candles.

"These are not good for the flow in here. You need to use real candles."

"I don't think so; they cost me a small fortune," he responds with that same amused laugh.

"You also need some plants in here and a fountain. The flow is all stopped up."

"I agree," his girlfriend says, cutting off Peter's exasperation.

Walking toward the back of the restaurant, closer to the bar area, feelings flood me and the letters S. M. burn into my eyes.

I turn to them. "I keep seeing the initials S. M. Who is S. M.? Do you know who that is?"

They shake their heads.

As I get closer to the bar, my breathing grows more labored and intense sensations rise in my body.

"S. M. S. M. I keep seeing S. M."

Still no response or recognition. Their noes and my insecurity about my gifts fly out the window. The puppet master is stealing the show.

"I'm also seeing the number 5. Does that mean anything to either of you?"

My questions continue to be met with blank stares.

As I get closer to the bar, I put my hand on my chest, peer around, stop, and stare. Lying on the floor is a man in a pool of blood. I look at them and then back down at the floor. The air in my lungs is as thick as mucus. I feel like I am drowning in my blood. The man on the floor wasn't a real person although I wouldn't put it past Peter; I was feeling mob ties. This was the ghost I was sensing.

"You have a man lying on the floor in a pool of blood!" I exclaim.

I stand above the spirit. Not afraid. The strange confidence takes over, and I don't care what I blurt out. This weird side of me is now becoming a "way of life."

"He has dark hair, is about 5'10", and is lying in a pool of blood."

"I keep seeing the initials S. M. and the number five. Does this mean anything to either of you?"

"No, they don't," Peter says, the grin becoming more sinister.

I am now on a mission to find out what is going on. Mediums read and feel everything at once. At least, I do. I hear, see, feel, and know, and most of the time, it all happens at once, so it's a wave of energy riding me, like a roller coaster. The roller coaster is heading directly toward the kitchen.

I step into the kitchen with the two of them in tow.

"There is a gray-haired woman here, who tells me she is the spirit's mother, and she's sticking around until we can move him along."

Blood and knives flood my vision.

"Did anyone cut themselves in the kitchen because I keep seeing knives and blood?"

Peter is adamant that no one cut themselves in the kitchen. The restaurant has only been open a month. He is the chef and runs a tight ship. As I walk around the kitchen, visions of blood and knives pervade my mind.

Then, the queasiness takes over. Bile rises in my throat. No wonder no one can eat here.

"We have to clear this place, and we need to start right here."

Finally, after journeying around the restaurant three times and clearing it, I sit down with Peter and his girlfriend for a chat. I have no control over all the information that continues to flood my brain, and I can't speak fast enough to get it out.

"I keep hearing the name Michael and seeing the initials S. M. Is that your partner's name?" I ask.

"No, I don't know a Michael."

"How about the number five? Does the number five mean anything to you?"

Again, he says no.

"I'm not sure this spirit wants to leave. I'm having a hard time moving him along."

I know Peter thinks I am trying to get more money out of him. He asks how much he owes me and ushers me out the door.

Standing on the sidewalk, now in the center of my life, I wonder what the heck just happened to me. Even though they can't confirm anything, I know what I saw was real. This is a turning point in my life, but I do not know where I am going. The puppet master and I get into my car, and I drive home.

A few weeks after the clearing, I get a call from Peter's girlfriend, asking if I can come back. They have confirmation. I ask her not to reveal anything to me as I like to work with pure energy.

The minute I step inside the restaurant and go to Peter and his girlfriend, the ghost is beside me.

He tells me his name is Sallie.

"Who is Sallie?" I ask. They look at me.

"Well, that is Sal Mineo," Peter answers.

I look perplexed. The name means nothing to me.

They share that the deceased guy behind the bar is Sal Mineo. Still, I have no clue who they are talking about, and the information continues.

"What is the number 37?"

"That is the age he was when he died."

"The wrong guy was convicted," I tell them.

They say they think so, too. Then, they fill me in a bit about what happened after I left. Five days later, a man named Michael came into the restaurant. He was a contractor and knew the businesses well in that line on Sunset Plaza. Sunset Plaza is a horseshoe. The businesses to the right do well but the ones to the left not so much. He shared with them that Sal Mineo had died in an alley that was a block away and in line with the restaurant.

And then the puppet master takes over, and I am flooded with information about the person who was convicted. I share everything I am getting.

For weeks, I work with Sal as he gives me information, and I deliver what I'm receiving to Peter. Then, Peter checks his sources and the internet and confirms things for me. I don't want to look Sal up and work only with him, but Sal and I continue to talk. He gives me information about who really killed him. Peter continues to piece together the information. Through my conversations with Sal, we discover who the actual killer may be.

Peter and I work like this for a while, and the events and communication are mind-blowing to everyone involved. We are all in awe. Sal is helping me to fully step out of skepticism and believe that we are, in fact, not alone. There is something happening in this world that is so much bigger than us. The puppet master hands me the strings, and I pull the moments of my own experience into view.

One day, I am giving a woman a reading in my apartment. I know nothing about her except her first name. In the reading, the guides reveal to me that she works in the entertainment industry. At the end of her reading, she shares how she knows all about me and Sal. Shocked, I ask, "How?" She explains that she is an executive for a movie company and that Peter is going around town pitching our story to movie executives.

Flabbergasted and upset that he is selling my story without my permission, I talk to an attorney. I learn my rights and approach Peter. I want to tell the true story and maybe write a book one day. Peter wants to make a movie and does not want to share or split anything with me. I explain that he does not own the rights to my story. We are at odds and go our separate ways.

I'm afraid to go at it alone. I realize that this Brooklyn Italian man is becoming comfortable to me and feeding the side of me that says I can't do it alone. Besides, Peter has the bravado, the connections, and the money to get this done. I don't.

Devastated, I keep talking to Sal and continue on, working on my own to piece together where the murder weapon might be. My guides give me information that Peter is trying to hire other mediums. Sal assures me he will work only with me. I talk to other mediums, and they repeat that Sal will only work with me. I hope this is true, but this is so new to me. I wonder, *Can I trust this information?*

I don't want Peter to tell the wrong story about Sal, who is someone I have come to love. I realize that he is another representation of an Italian man, but this one, although dead, is loving and kind. I feel so bad that I am disappointing Sal and promise to continue to work with him, even though I feel like I don't have the resources or money to find the weapon and interview the possible murderer.

Eventually, Peter calls and asks to meet me at the restaurant. I agree because I want to help Sal. This precious life has entrusted me with his story. *I wonder what Peter will say. What does he want?*

Arriving on time, I sit in the back near the bar, which is now named "Sal's Bar." Peter is running late—one of his tactics. He swaggers in and sits across from me, and after talking for a bit, he asks me to work with him again, promising me that it will be 50/50 in everything. He will include me in meetings with cops and share all the information with me.

We shake hands.

He leans in and whispers, "Hey, is Sal here? He hasn't been around since you left."

I can't believe what I'm hearing. Sal told me he wouldn't communicate with anyone but me.

I look at Peter and ask, "What do you mean?"

"I haven't felt him since you were here last, and I'm wondering if he is still around," he explains.

"Oh, he's here with me now and has been with me ever since." I smirk, get up, and leave.

As I sit in my car, tears pour out of me. I shake my head in disbelief. This spirit has my back more than most people I know. I realize Sal is the one who sent the Hollywood executive to my house to alert me of what was going on behind my back. Now, he confirms that he refuses to talk to other mediums—only me. Sal taught me that loyalty and love transcend all time. Sal taught me to believe.

Marilyn Alauria

PART THREE

*Deepening Your Connection
with Your Guides*

For things to reveal themselves to us,
we need to be ready to abandon our views about them.

—THICH NHAT HANH

PRACTICES TO DEEPEN YOUR RELATIONSHIP WITH YOUR GUIDES

$\blacklozenge$

I n this life, you are dancing with the universe, and everything is information for you. When you're vibing with the universe, you're realizing, *Oh, that's why the birds showed up. Oh, that's why there's a yes here. Oh, that's why I don't really like that teacher.* Even the "no" answers you receive are for your greater good. Everything is information for your personal journey—your soul—and your guides are here to help communicate that knowledge to you.

Your relationship with your guides is a deep and personal experience. They're building trust with you. It's like going on a date with someone. You're starting to get to know them. You don't build that relationship overnight. It can happen quickly, but it's still a relationship. As you develop your connection, you get to know them on an intimate level.

To know what form your guides may take, start with how you feel. What inspires your love? Ascended beings, nature, the moon? Whatever answer you decide is your guide, because you've picked it, and they've picked you. It is an intimate relationship that is meaningful to you. You are in co-creation, and your relationship grows with your guide, just like your relationship grows with a loved one.

When your guides are communicating with you, it's important to remember they are not "in a box." You can't meet your guides in a box. All souls are creative, and guides are the true essence of creativity. They will communicate with you using imaginative means. I encourage you to stay open and practice using all your intuitive senses to expand your experience with your guides.

My guides are creative teachers. I'd like to share with you some of their tools, so you can have a meaningful, deep, beautiful, and loving relationship with your guide. This relationship will help you to live the life you are meant to live—a life you love.

BREATHE WITH YOUR GUIDES

One of the best ways to start communicating with your guides is through your breath. Your breath was given to you because it's Divinity, it's God, it's the Universe; it's your existence. Your breath is what makes you unique, and it is intimate to you.

First, pick a guide to work with. If you don't have a guide, then pick an ascended being, an angel, someone famous you admire who is deceased, or an animal. I usually suggest you don't work with a deceased loved one right away because people sometimes struggle with hearing their loved ones in their new consciousness. They confuse it with their memories of the person, and therefore, it can be difficult to truly hear them.

Do you have your guide? Remember to trust and not overthink it.

Now close your eyes and ask that guide to come forward. Tell them to stand in a particular place near you. They may already be standing somewhere; you decide if that feels good for you. They want you to decide. Remember, this is a co-creative relationship. You get to have feelings and opinions about how you would like to do this work. Notice the distance that feels comfortable to you. Are they five feet away or twenty feet? It doesn't matter; it's whatever feels good to you.

Now inhale, and as you exhale, send them your breath. Feel them taking your breath as they inhale, and when they exhale, they send their breath back to you. By the second breath, when you are inhaling, you are taking in breath from them. When you exhale, you are sending them breath. Do this for about five breaths. On the sixth breath, when you send them your breath, send them a color with it. See it as a line of colored energy. When they breathe back to you, that color is getting stronger. As you continue to breathe with them, that color becomes a line of energy like an umbilical cord, connecting you to your guides.

Notice how you feel. This is so important. People forget to feel, and it's one of the biggest ways our guides communicate with us.

When you feel ready, you can open your eyes. How did that feel?

If you didn't feel your guide, don't worry. There is nothing wrong with you. You are learning a new language. Do it again. Play with the location and color if you want. The important word here is "play." You don't learn a new language in ten minutes; it takes time.

Remember to surrender and trust. The more you do this, the more you will feel your guides.

SYMBOLIC LANGUAGE OF THE SOUL

Your "clairs" are how you see, hear, feel, sense, and know—how you receive information. The Symbolic Language of the Soul is a way to discern the deeper meaning and the message for you. As you experience the diverse ways to connect with your guides, a better understanding of their unique message for you is key.

We've seen guides speak through different forms. One of the best ways to open to their communication is by using your life experiences and feelings to interpret the symbol and message your guides have specifically shown you.

We all have had a variety of experiences in our lives. Even people raised in the same family by the same parents experience life differently. We were different ages when things happened in the family; therefore, our experiences and memories may differ from those of a sibling or parent. For example, if your father came home and told you that he got a new job that would require your family to move, you might have been thrilled because you didn't like the school you were in, but your sister, who loved her school, would have had a different response to that news.

No one else has experienced what you have; they haven't read the same books, dated the same people, or had the same friends. No one else has the perspective you have. You are unique, and your guides know it. That is why they send you certain symbols. They know that symbol will carry a message to you that is different from what your sister or the person sitting next to you would perceive.

The Symbolic Language of the Soul is a technique to help you interpret the symbol without the need for Google or books. With that said, there is nothing wrong with looking something up. There are great internet sites and books out there to inform you. Heck, you're reading one right now, aren't you? But have you run to Google to look up a symbol and had tons of sites come up? You don't know which one to pick, so you just pick one. You read it, and you are disappointed by what it says, or you are unsure what it means regarding your life. Sometimes, the message might even scare you.

Your guides are asking you to find your personal identity and language so when you receive a message, you can understand what your truth is. In that way, you can have a unique experience with your understanding of the symbol and not somebody else's experience of it. You decide on the best thing for you. To me, that is the key to your soul and your journey.

SYMBOLIC LANGUAGE OF YOUR SOUL EXERCISE

For this exercise, you need to have a piece of paper and a pen to write down your questions and answers. Writing them down gives you information to go back to and reflect.

First, think of a question you may have. Do not ask a yes or no question. Ask a question that requires a more expansive answer. Trust the first question that comes to your mind.

Now, answer my question: "What does butterfly mean to you?"

Try to write more than one word.

After you answer, close your eyes, and see a butterfly.

"How does it make you feel?"

Write it down.

"Do you have a memory of butterflies?"

If so, write that down. Don't worry if you don't have a memory about it; you are still doing great.

Now, let's build on this exercise. We will pick one more symbol.

"What does a candle mean to you?"

Write down more than one word.

Close your eyes and see a candle.

"How do you feel?"

Write it down.

Next, trust and have fun with your imagination. Close your eyes and see what you get, or take the first thing that comes to mind.

The candle is giving you a song. "What song is it?"

If you don't get a song, guess because you can't get this wrong.

Write your answer down.

Now, listen to the song and read the lyrics.

Pull out some of the lyrics and write it on your paper.

At the end, read your questions and answers aloud. Even if you didn't get a complete answer, trust me. By doing this exercise, you are one step closer to your answer. Pay attention for the next twenty-four to forty-eight hours, because information will be coming your way. If you get another symbol, do this exercise again.

ARE YOU MAKING IT UP?

When I first started communicating with my guides, I thought, *How do I know I'm not just making this up?*

They replied, *We're giving you great advice; who cares?*

They're right, I thought. Without delay, they gave me permission to move forward.

In the beginning, it's more important for you to learn how to communicate with your guides than to worry about what's right, what's wrong, or what you are making up.

This technique will help you know whether you are making this up. First, I'll explain what I used, and then I will walk you through the exercise. To do this exercise, I used a mini-me. She looked like me, was ballsy like me, and was definitely no-nonsense.

I had a conversation with mini-me and asked her to sit on my right shoulder. While I was channeling with my guides, if I questioned the information, I would turn my attention to mini-me, who was on my right shoulder, and ask her if I was manipulating. She would have to answer honestly. She agreed, and we made a pact. She now had a job. The next time I was channeling, she was right there on my right shoulder, waiting for when I needed her.

When I got to a question that I cared deeply about, I found I couldn't trust the answer I was receiving. I asked her if I was manipulating, and she said, *Nope, your fine.*

I worked with her for about a year. Sometimes, she would say I was manipulating, and sometimes, she would say I wasn't. I trusted her response no matter what she said. This taught me how to know my guides and their energy in their responses. I got to know them so well that I no longer needed mini-me, because I would very rarely manipulate a response. I knew my guides so well that I no longer questioned their answers. You can do this, too.

You can choose to use your mini-me or pick a cartoon character or animal to sit on your shoulder or somewhere near you. I'd suggest you choose whatever you feel you can trust. I needed that no-nonsense side of me to keep me in line. You may need an owl or something else. When you pick what you want to work with, close your eyes and do a self-guided meditation in which you meet them and discuss how you would like them to work with you.

Be sure to pick one word or phrase as your check, whether it's manipulating, making it up, trusting, or a phrase of your own. Stay with the same word or phrase so you can build trust in the process. Make a pact with your mini-me (or whatever you choose) and ask that they answer honestly. Then promise yourself you will trust the response.

Decide where they will be during your meditation. Will they sit on your shoulder or in your heart? It doesn't matter. You get to choose. Remember, you are the instrument, so it has to feel good to you.

If you pick something and don't fully trust they will answer you honestly, pick something else. If you don't trust they will answer you honestly, you might have chosen the wrong thing. Keep trying until you find one that works. You will find it, and it won't take long. Usually, it's the first thing you choose.

LEARN TO TRUST YOUR GUIDES

This is an easy one—one that I have taught thousands of people, and when they truly do it, they are blown away. Before I share it, do you pinky swear to do it, to commit to it? If you feel a resounding yes throughout your system, then you are ready for this exercise.

It's important to promise to do the exercise for thirty days, no matter what is happening in your life. Wake up saying to your guides: "I promise to trust you for thirty days."

Go to sleep saying you promise to trust them. You can even count down the days, but you must do it for thirty days. It works. It's amazing. Let me tell you a quick story.

When I was looking for my second home, I was searching in an area with little inventory. There was only one house available in my price range. I was about to put an offer in when my guides said to wait until Monday. I was scared and didn't want to wait because I was cutting it close to when I needed to move. Again, they repeated, *Wait until Monday.*

So, I did, and that Monday, two more houses in my range came on the market. When I went to see the houses, I found the one I wanted. The market was extremely competitive, and I was going to bid high. My guides told me to wait again. They said more houses would come on the market that week.

It was Saturday, and again, I was afraid to wait. They repeated their information, and I trusted them. Five more houses came on the market in that area. Even my realtor expressed shock at the number of houses that popped up on the market. My guides were right. I got the house I loved and paid almost the price my guides told me. I had let people talk me into a higher price, even though I knew the person who bid against me.

"Why'd you bid so high? You knew I couldn't go above a certain amount," he said.

I knew it. My guides knew it. I trust my guides. If I had stayed in fear and didn't trust them, I wouldn't be writing this book from my home, looking out at the beautiful redwoods.

What do you have to lose by trusting your guides for thirty days?

IMAGINATION IS EVERYTHING

Years ago, when I first started studying about guides, there were antiquated teachers telling us not to use our imaginations. They said imagination was bad, which meant we weren't doing it right. That felt wrong to me because my guides encouraged me to use my imagination. They told me that is where they are. They said that all souls are creative, and guides want you to be creative. Use your imagination. That is where magic is happening.

I record all my sessions with my guides. I have hundreds upon hundreds of recordings. I don't remember all of my sessions with them. If there is something they want me to remember, I will. Sometimes, I will write an important piece of information down as soon as I come out of a meditation with my guides.

One day, I had to make a big decision about my life and I felt lost. I went for a walk and brought one of my recorders with me. This recorder had more than six files on it with up to fourteen or more recordings in each file. I hadn't used the recorder in a while, so I had no idea what year the recordings were from.

My guides told me to listen to recording number seven in file number three. Not even knowing if this one had seven recordings on it, I trusted and went to that recording and listened. I was amazed by what my guides had told me about my life a year prior. Everything had come true—from going into a yoga program that I didn't even know existed at the time to deciding on my move. After listening to that recording, I knew to trust my guides, and I knew what decision I needed to make.

Had I worried about getting it right or not using my imagination because I might be making it up, I wouldn't be where I am today, teaching all of you and living a beautiful life. Please, use your imagination and play with your guides.

Let's use your imagination right now; read below.

IMAGINATION EXERCISE

Think of a question you have. Try not to make it a yes or no question. Yes or no questions can be fine, but sometimes, they can limit a bigger response your guides want to give. Try asking a question about what you need to know or where you need to go.

For example: What do I need to know about _____? What do I need to know about myself to grow into _____? Where do I need to go to find out more about _____? You get the idea.

Now, ask a question.

Once you have your question, trust your imagination. Go with your first response.

Pick or see a flower in your mind's eye. It doesn't matter if you close your eyes and see the flower or if you choose one. Either works.

What kind of flower is it?

What color is it?

How does it make you feel?

Write down the color and how you feel.

Now pick or see an animal.

What animal do you see?

What character traits does the animal have? Name three.

Next, the animal gives you the name of a famous person. Remember, use your imagination.

What famous person did you receive? Do you know the person?

What do you like about the person?

Write it down.

I always ask secret questions when I play these games, so follow along.

You had a question. Write the question down and write down all the answers you got.

What color was the flower?

The color represents a chakra that you might need to work with to find a solution to this question. Spend time in this chakra, breathing into it, asking your question, and trusting you will get the answer.

For me, the colors and the meanings of the chakras are as follows:

- **Root Chakra:** Red—belief systems, spiritual truths, and abundance
- **Sacral Chakra:** Orange—creativity
- **Solar Plexus Chakra:** Yellow—intuition
- **Heart Chakra:** Green—empathic ability and following your truth
- **High Heart Chakra:** Pink—compassion for self
- **Throat Chakra:** Blue—clairaudience and speaking your truth
- **Third Eye Chakra:** Indigo—clairvoyance, using your imagination, and seeing your truth
- **Crown Chakra:** White or Lavender—connection to your guides and the Divine

How did you feel when you saw the flower?

The answer is representative of how you feel about the answer that is coming to you. If you are feeling love, great. If you are fearful, that is great, too. There are no right or wrong answers. Everything is information.

What animal did you pick?

What were its character traits?

These are the traits you will open up to fully step into the power of this answer.

What famous person did they give you and why?

These are the traits you can lean into to gather courage to move forward. Now look up famous quotes by the person and go deeper.

If you are still unclear about the answer, I will teach you one of my favorite lessons from my guides: the dot.dot.dot technique.

DOT.DOT.DOT TECHNIQUE

This was one of the most profound lessons my guides ever taught me. When you get an answer, don't put a period at the end of it. Instead, put a dot.dot.dot and ask more questions. Let me explain.

If you ask your guide a question, and they give you the color blue, don't sit there and think, *I got the color blue, period!* Instead, ask more questions.

Why did they give me the color blue?

What do I feel about the color blue?

What does blue remind me of?

Do I have a memory of blue?

The question possibilities are endless. Be the investigator of your own life. Answer these questions with your own life experience. You will be closer to the answer to your question, and you will be on a journey to something even greater than you can imagine.

The dot.dot.dot technique allows you to open up to solutions that are so much bigger than your thinking. It allows your guides to perform their magic and show you what is possible. It's possible that you are not ready for the exact answer, because you have to learn something about yourself, build up a character trait, or get ready to receive an even greater opportunity. Your life has so much potential. Why end that potential with a period?

USE A PHYSICAL OBJECT

Remember, I said people complicate things. It's true. It's okay. I put my guides to task, too. But let's try a fun tool that will take you from not trusting to communicating.

Sometimes it's hard to see a guide, a mini-me, or a color in front of you. I suggest you work with a physical object and breathe with it. Pick a physical object that you like and hold it in your hands. Now, using the object do the breathing exercise above with your eyes open. Breathe with the object. Send it breath and feel breath come from it. Everything is energy, and your guides are energy, too.

Breathe back and forth with the object. Then take the color of the object and use that for the line of energy. Notice how you feel as you take energy from the object. You may feel your heart opening, your breath becoming easier, or your throat chakra opening.

Now, focus on one spot on the object; let that area become bigger. Feel it becoming bigger than the object. Let it communicate to you. What does it feel like? What does it want you to know? Use your imagination and trust it.

Now try it with your eyes closed. Imagine you see the object and do the whole exercise again. Does the information grow? Are your senses sharper?

This is a wonderful way to practice using yourself as the instrument. I'm not telling you what you want to feel, see, or hear. You are allowing the experience to happen to you. This will help you develop your innate psychic skills.

For example, when I do this exercise with my water bottle, the blue overtakes me and tells me to trust I am exactly where I need to be, and I can't agree more. In a channel session, one woman was using a bottle of water, and the information that was flooding through was incredible for her because she was able to see something tangible.

Holding a physical object releases the mind chatter, the random thoughts that can stop us. When you stay focused on an object, you will receive profound results.

COLOR YOUR GUIDES

One of the best ways to remove expectations of who you think your guide is and what you think of your guide is to color them. This technique allows you to connect with them in your own way. It's one of the most magical tools I can give you.

Grab your paints, crayons, or pastels. Anything you fancy will work. Take your paper, find a lovely place to sit, and light a candle if you like. Now breathe, and let's use your imagination.

Close your eyes and do the breathing technique with your guide. After you have done that, choose a color and put it on the paper. Don't worry about drawing a person or an object; just play with putting color on the paper. Now and then, stop to look at what you have drawn; take it in, close your eyes, and breathe with your guide. Then start coloring some more. You can repeat the above process until you feel done. You will know when your task is complete.

Look at what you drew. How does it feel? Take it in.

For extra credit, you can breathe with the picture with your eyes open and deepen the relationship with your guide. You also can stare at the picture, close your eyes, see it in your third eye, make it life-size, and step into it or communicate with it. When you have finished, you can step out of it and shrink it back to size.

If there's a being that you feel connected to but you don't know what they look like, color them. When you color them, you have an automatic connection because our souls are composed of color and light and sound.

SOUND

Sound is another way for us to get out of the practical mind—the practical way of thinking—so we are better able to communicate with our guides in a pure form. Our souls vibrate and they are naturally drawn to sound and color. If I look at my soul, I can see a specific color, I can see a shape, and I can feel the energy, or vibration, of it. When I tune in deeper, I can make a sound, and that would be the personal language of my soul.

To practice, feel a guide in front of you and open your mouth without saying words; just project a sound to your guide. If I was going to make a sound for that moment, my sound may be "Aaaaaa."

Your sound will be different. It is going to be a personal language that you and your guide are going to have.

Now say it aloud. Feel the sound traveling out of your mouth and see it going back into your ear. You are now open to hearing in a unique and wonderful way. Do this for a bit and feel the vibration of the sound in your body. Now, send this sound to your guide and listen: did they send you a sound back? If they do, repeat that sound back to them. You are creating a sound vibration session between the two of you.

NUMBERS

As I mentioned before, numbers are infinite. They have so many meanings. When they appear, you have to consider what you were thinking of, what questions you have been asking your guides, and how you feel. Here are the initial meanings of the numbers from zero to ten.

- **Zero**: Infinity, loving cycle, taking a good risk. Experiencing your soul's joy.
- **One**: New beginnings in your life and on your journey. Trusting yourself.
- **Two**: Partnership with self, your soul, and others. These partnerships could be romantic, business, friends, or family. Also, the need to be creative.
- **Three**: Mind, body, and soul connection. Coming into completion. Fullness. Trusting your intuition.
- **Four**: Building new foundations and belief systems. Making money through spiritual truths. Could also represent heart-opening experiences.
- **Five**: Transformation. Change. Speaking your truth.
- **Six**: Family and friends and moving into or out of a community. Also, seeing things for what they are.
- **Seven**: Developing psychic ability. Opening up to channel. Trusting your spirit guides.
- **Eight**: Business, infinity, heaven. Connection to higher dimensions.
- **Nine**: End of a cycle. Soul number. Entering a new way of being. A new consciousness.
- **Ten**: Goes back to one but can be new beginnings multiplied. Guidance by Infinite Intelligence.

What happens when you see more than one number? If the same number appears in threes or fours, it means it's powerful, and there is a meaningful message coming through. In tarot, when you receive three major arcana cards in a three-card reading, it means there is a substantial change happening in your life. The cards will reveal what that change is. It's the same with numbers. If you see the same number frequently, a big message is coming through.

The numbers that people report seeing repeatedly are 333 or 444 or 1111 or 5555. How would you read these numbers? Read the numbers individually and then add them up, read that number, and then break it down to a single digit, and read that number.

Let's take 444 for example. First, you know it's a 4, which is building new foundations and belief systems and making money through spiritual truths. The number 4 could also represent heart-opening experiences.

Then, you do the equation 4+4+4=12, and you break the answer down to 1 and 2. The number 1 is new beginnings in your life and on your journey; it also represents trusting yourself. The number 2 is partnership with self, your soul, and others. These partnerships could be romantic, business, friends, or family. This number also is the need to be creative.

Then, you take the 12 and break it down to a single digit by doing the equation 1+2=3. The number three is mind, body, and soul connection, coming into completion, fullness, and trusting your intuition.

If this number came up in a reading, I would summarize it this way: You are making huge changes in your life and shifting your belief systems. What you once knew to be true is changing. Through this change, you are going to have a heart-opening experience and quite possibly find a new career, which will lead to new beginnings and partnerships with people you align with. This experience is leading you to wholeness and will help you to complete one area of your life and expand into a new way of being.

Now, you try it. Think of a question and pick a number. It can be a three-digit number with all the numbers being the same, or it can be three random numbers. Write down the three-digit number and the meanings next to them. Then, say it aloud and add whatever else you might like to add. There isn't a science to any of this. The more you allow your imagination to flow, the more the numbers will come alive and speak to you.

Remember to have fun.

BOUNDARIES AND EXPECTATIONS

This is huge. You must have boundaries with your guides. Think about it. Do you meet someone and let them do whatever they want to you? I hope not. Your guides want you to tell them how you would like them to work with you. By doing so, you create a bond with them and learn how to trust each other.

When I first started working with my guides, I told them they couldn't just come in whenever they wanted. I wanted to live a normal life and didn't want to know information about other people or situations. It just wasn't for me. So, I gave them boundaries for when they could come through. They respected my boundaries and we learned to trust each other.

After about six years, they told me they needed to come through whenever they wanted. I didn't know why, but I trusted them and said okay. They were preparing me for what was to come next. Soon after they asked to do this, I was in discussions around Hollywood about having my own show. I had meetings with different networks for which I had to go in and be me and then launch into readings. My guides were with me the whole time.

You decide what works for you and tell them. Then, work with them and grow your relationship. There will come a time when you can be in constant communication, and it will enhance your life.

I encourage you to play with these tools and techniques and make them your own. My guides take from every corner of my life, mix it with magic, and create tools and techniques I can share with everyone.

Dive back into these exercises with your guides, take from the corners of your own life experiences, and create a powerful tool chest of your own. You will be surprised what you can create to open the passageway to communication with your guides. That thing you learned in history class, on the basketball court, or from that cab driver suddenly comes dancing into your awareness; mix it with a new color of your own, and bam, you are in your own personal conversation with your guides, using the most important instrument known to God—you!

From the first moment I met my guides, I have been growing my relationship with them. It never stays the same. Our relationship, the way we communicate, my gifts, my teaching, and what I'm meant to do continues to evolve because they're infinite. It can be the same for you.

PURE ESSENCE MEETS PURE ESSENCE

———◆———

So many people put their guides on a pedestal. They bow down to them, not realizing that their guides are here to co-create with them. We do not need to revere them as if they're higher than us. When we do that, we judge ourselves as a soul. Our guides will never judge us as a soul.

As I mentioned in the previous chapter, our relationship is fluid and continues to grow and change. You grow and change. Neither you nor the relationship can grow and evolve if you bow down to your guides and are not participating in the creation of your relationship.

When I started bowing down to my guides, they started bowing down to me.

Whoa, what's going on here? I asked.

You don't recognize that you're helping us to do what we need to do in our consciousness on the other side, they said.

There's a mutual back-and-forth of helping each other at such a deep level that it makes our relationship more intimate than we can even understand. To help, I can give you a handbook and tools to communicate and invite you to bring your soul—your instrument—into the conversation. Then, sit back and let the exciting adventure begin.

Guides transcend time and space. They can be in many different places and dimensions simultaneously, waiting for us to take their hand and invite them into the dance.

If we look at the dimensions as a type of energy, we've already done this dance together in several types of energy. We have a dynamic relationship—pure essence meets pure essence—and we work together. That is why it's imperative that you recognize that you are more than worthy of this type of engagement. It is your birthright. Life is calling you out onto the dance floor—the dance of your soul in deeper connection with your guides. Get to know them. You have known them before.

Throughout time or different incarnations, you might have walked the Earth plane with your guides as physical beings. They also might have been your guide in other lifetimes. They could be your guides in future lifetimes. You can also switch places with your guides. You could have been or can be a guide for one or more of your guides. The relationship is two ways. It's not just that we're the ones in the physical world, and they're a higher dimensional being that's helping us. We are in a relationship with them, and we also support them.

Seeing our Divinity as spiritual beings empowers us to understand that we can be guides for others. Our pure essence as consciousness—our soul—may have a type of expertise that helps our guides in their own lives. I have guided my main guide through a specific growth moment in her life. It wasn't an earthly existence; it was something else. Because of that, she's been indebted to me, but not in a way in which she bows down to me. We simply have reverence for each other. She can bring her light to my existence and help me accelerate my growth.

Our guides can also be guides for other people because they can be in multiple places at once. What's important is that our guides are aware of and respect our relationship and our human experience. They work with what helps us grow.

Personally, I would not want my guides to be guides for other people. As the only daughter, I would have had a tough time accepting my mother loving another girl as much as she loved me. It's the same for my relationship with my guides. Other people may be fine with their guides working with other people. Our guides will do whatever best serves our purposes.

However, if we can be open to our guides helping other people, it brings more into our lives. Whenever someone helps another, they're accelerating, growing, and learning. When our guides support others, they bring more intelligence and infinite expansion into our experiences.

Writing this, I can accept that my guides might need to work with other people and something that was foreign and uncomfortable to me just a few sentences earlier has shifted in a nanosecond. That is what this work does for us. It helps us recognize that there is no scarcity or lack; there is only infinite intelligence, love, support, and fun.

I love being on this ride with my guides. They have made my life colorful, magical, fun, and intuitive. They are a profound expression of my soul. There is no denying that I live fully in every aspect of my life. I am fully present, fully engaged, and fully ready to be a spiritual being walking a human existence with unseen beings supporting me. I invite you to do the same.

FINAL THOUGHTS AND BLESSINGS

---◆---

knew I wasn't alone. I felt open and ready to receive.

Oh, what a journey this has been. I feel like you were with me from the first word I wrote and will continue to be with me after I write the last chapter. Guides teach us that we are all one. There is no separation. There never was.

Our guides are innovative and miraculous. Our relationship with them completes our relationship with ourselves. Oh, what can be and is. Can you feel into that? What can be, *is!*

As a number one priority, guides answer the questions inside of us. They help us remember who we are and why we are here, even if we don't understand that is what they're doing. And remembering who we are brings us home to ourselves, which, for most people, leads to peace, comfort, encouragement, and serenity.

A long time ago, before I met my first guide, I set out to achieve three big dreams in my life. The first two I received right away, but the third one eluded me. I didn't understand why, but I had my first two dreams to occupy my time. Still, I wondered what I needed to do to find my third dream—inner peace.

Shortly after that, my first two accomplishments went away, leaving me feeling dumbstruck. How could I have achieved my dreams—what I desired—just to have it go away? That experience took me on a journey—a journey to my guides and to inner peace. My guides knew what they were doing, back before I even met them. They knew what they were doing when they entered my life. I didn't—but they did. They knew I would learn that I was not alone and that there is always something greater than me out there.

My guides taught me how to trust them—to lean back in my chair into thin air and feel them always supporting me, guiding me. I learned to love myself for all of who I am and to accept myself fully. My guides taught me to believe in the dreams in my heart and in myself. They give me the courage to live my greatest life, whispering in my ear when I need encouragement and tapping me on my back when I need to move along.

They have taught me to take what I love—my communication with them—and introduce it to others. I have learned to invite people in to find their own language with their guides—not my language, but their own personal language, their own instrument. I want to help others to develop their intimate connection with their guides and discover the love that I know exists for all of us.

We are all magical creations—gifted and special. My guides brought me home to my soul, which has brought me inner peace. Now you have the techniques and tools to do the same. Go out there and live boldly, in full acceptance of yourself. Take the risks you desire, follow the dreams in your heart, and know you are never, ever alone. Your guides have your back, and they are with you every step of the way.

APPENDIX

Pick Your Guide

PICK YOUR GUIDE

Here's a fun exercise for you. These guides were given to me by my guides, and they want to offer them to you.

First, think of something you would love to work on. Put your hands on your heart and close your eyes. Think of your question and pick a number from 1 to 10. After you do this, open your eyes, find your number, and meet your guide.

1—MARTAR: DREAM BIG

Martar teaches you to be creative in your life and live the life of your dreams. What destiny have you been waiting to create? Your gifts are your treasure. Open your heart and let your gifts flow. You came here to do great things and now is your time. Stop waiting for people to give you permission. What permission do you need to give yourself? Give yourself that permission and make a solid plan with Martar today. Then, commit to taking the first step toward your dream and mark it on your calendar. If it's not on your calendar, it's not getting done. Take the first step toward your dreams. Martar tells you to stand tall and dream big!

2—OSEN: ARTFUL FLOW

Osen embodies both masculine and feminine energy. No matter what is going on in your life or where you want to go, Osen will grab at you and pull you in the direction of your dreams. Osen wants you to write the story in your heart, even if it is just for yourself. They open the door for you and invite you to travel in time. Step out of any disappointment and misery into feeling fulfilled. They believe in you more than you do. You are asked to write a new story—the one you want to live. What new story do you want to write and share? Osen invites you into an artful flow.

3—STRELL: SHINE BRIGHTLY WITH POSSIBILITY

Strell helps you believe in impossible dreams. She knows that nothing is out of your reach, and all you have to do is be honest with yourself about what you want, ask for it, and then take inspired action. Strell reminds you that you are a bright star, and it's time for you to let your light shine. See the light shine on the path in front of you. What steps toward your dreams will you take on that path today? It's time to breathe new possibilities into your life. Commit to creating change by taking a step today. Strell encourages you to shine brightly with possibility.

4—TRAY: EXPANSION

Tray teaches you how to reconnect to yourself using nature and feeling the Divine run through your breath. Ask yourself what dance is in your heart and dance. Tray invites you to open the doors to other lifetimes, where you achieved magical things. He holds all the tools you need to create a full life while you are here on earth. He gives you the courage to live the life you were meant to live. Whatever tool you need to do it, he's handing it to you now. Tray invites you to take action and live a life full of expansion.

5—BLEE: PROMISE OF A NEW SPECTACULAR VIEW

Believe in your dreams. You are a golden gift from the world. What you need to move forward is to believe in your magic. Blee helps you to remember who you are and why you came here. She connects you to your soul, so you have organic responses that lead you down the path to living your truth—the truth you were meant to live not the one handed down to you. She whispers in your ear that you are poetry in motion. Be the poem you wish to live. What are you going to put into motion today? What do you want to believe today? Blee gives you the promise of a new spectacular view.

6—WENDR: BALANCE

No matter what your fear, whisper it to Wendr, and he will take it away and replace it with love. He will remind you of who you truly are—a Divine, magical being, who is destined to live the life in your heart. How can you invite in abundance today? Time travel is something he loves to guide you through. That abundant life you dream of is a parallel life (it's happening now), and Wendr can help you live the life you are dreaming about. He believes in you more than you do. He invites you to shift into believing in yourself as much as he does. He knows that can only happen if you take a step out into the world and own your beautiful voice and soul. Wendr offers you balance to feel the unseen love he offers with the love you have for yourself.

7—LAYU: SING THE SONG OF YOUR SOUL

Layu helps you know that your wishes are coming true. You need to take flight and see the world from an expanded view—to know that you have always been okay, and you will always be okay. What do you want to be known for? That ache in your heart is not from the hurt you experienced but from the life, you are not living. The dreams you have swallowed down are pushing up against the walls of your heart, asking to be released. That aching in your heart needs to be heard. What song in your heart needs to be sung? Layu dares you to be adventurous and sing the song of your soul.

8—HONTAS: INNER PEACE

Hontas is a healer—a medicine woman of all things. Immerse yourself in all things spiritual, whatever spiritual means to you. It's time to breathe revival into your life. What do you want to heal? Like all great medicine women, find your tribe. Don't stand around asking where they are. Tell Hontas what kind of people you want to be surrounded by. She knows the community that can support you and help build you up when you are down. With a staff in your hand, being the innate pathfinder you are, head out into the horizon in search of your community. Hontas calls you out of the shadows and asks you to move boldly and a sense of inner peace will fill you as you journey.

9—SPREE: CREATIVE PLAY

Spree encourages you to create, create, and create some more. You are creative. Your soul is creative and doesn't believe anything but that to be true. Weave the world you want to live. Look at your life as a beautiful tapestry. Look at past experiences as weaving beautiful colors into your soul. You would not be who you are today had you not gotten to experience disappointment, sadness, great joys, and love in your life. You are a story in motion. Bask in joy and bring it to others through the art of creative play. What creativity would you like to bring into your life? Spree asks you to commit to doing something you love today.

10—BLITHE: BELIEVE

Blithe is always looking out for you from above. He teaches you to listen to your inner guidance, trust your heart, and soar into your dreams. He feels that nothing is impossible, and he asks that you believe in the impossible. Blithe reminds you that when it feels like the world is giving you a no, it's really a *yes* in disguise. There is something so much more magical than you can ever have imagined because you dream with brackets on. You dream from the past. Look ahead and make a promise to yourself today that you are going to grow in all areas of your life, health, relationships, and career. What impossible thing do you want to do? Blithe encourages to you believe that you are meant to do it.

You have met your guide, and you have the book to help you communicate with them. Talk to them, use the tools I've given you, and co-create a magical life together.

MEET OUR SACRED STORYTELLERS

ANDREA ANDREE lives in Wisconsin with her husband and beautiful star seeds, Mara and Dean. Andrea recently re-discovered her empathic nature and spiritual gifts and is following the call to use her gifts as a coach and healer, helping other moms discover who they are after kids. andreaandree. com.

SUMITA BANERJEA, PH.D. is an educator, author, and counselor. Sumita has written text books for schools and conducts workshops for teachers and students.

CAROL CAMPOS is a heart-centered consultant, writer, and life mentor, focusing on empowerment, self-awareness, and manifestation. She is passionate about acceptance and belonging in all areas of life. carolelizabethco.com.

SUJON DATTA is an internationally renowned life architect, bioenergetic healer, and spiritual advisor. Sujon's mission is to help people open their hearts to themselves to reach their highest potential.

JENNIFER HERRERA has been practicing energetic healing arts and bodywork for 10+ years. Jennifer is a reiki master, and a certified coach through HeartMath, Inc. seaandstonewellness.com.

JENNIFER K. HILL is an author, speaker, TV & radio host, entrepreneur and thought leader. She has hosted popular shows with Dr. Deepak Chopra, Dr. Rollin McCraty, and many others. om-heals.com.

TAMARA KNOX, PH.D., D.D. is an international bestselling author and enthusiast of Theocentric Psychology. Her passion is to embody the primordial essence of sound, movement, food energetics, breath, and consciousness. Tamara's dedication to multidimensional Oneness allows her to express, write, and inhabit joy through life and challenging times. shekhinahpath.com.

LARA JAEGER is just a regular person who has had an extraordinary experience. Lara is the mother of three children and works entirely from the comfort of her home.

PATRISHE MAXWELL was raised in Dublin, Ireland and has a deep connection to the Druid Path and her Celtic roots. She is passionate about working with women and children who have experienced feeling unwanted, unloved, and abandoned.

DEBI MENZER is a mom, social worker, animal rescuer, and student of all things Divine and mysterious.

SUSAN B. MERCER is a bestselling author, award winning producer, end of life advocate, interior designer, and spiritual alchemist. Her ability to connect with individuals enables her to assist many clients through their life transitions with clarity, thoughtfulness, and love. modernoutlooks.com.

MARIA NORDIN has a deep love for Mother Earth and it is in nature she feels most alive and connected. Maria likes to work with symbols and the mysterious magic of life.

MAYLIN LUE PANN attributes her faith in God for her ability to triumph over adversity, including regrouping after a failed franchise and surviving cancer twice.

SANDRA PELLEY endured sixteen years of injuries, chronic pain, and suicidal thoughts. Her guides were yelling at her to make changes. Then it happened… the light at the end of the tunnel. Sandra discovered her most intimate guide, her Little You, learned to ask for help and changed her thoughts to find the silver linings. sandrapelley.com.

DR. ANDREA PENNINGTON is an integrative physician, acupuncturist, bestselling author, TEDx speaker and creator of The Attunement Meditation. She facilitates workshops which promote holistic healing, resilience, trauma recovery and self-love. andreapennington.com.

JENNIFER PEREZ SOLAR is a Samassati colorlight practitioner, newborn care specialist, and teacher. Her psychic and mediumship gifts merge with her business expertise to show others how to be change agents and movement creators. allowandflow.com.

CHRISTY PERRY is the founder and owner of The BhakTee Life. An accomplished sound practitioner, Christy works with Tibetan and crystal singing bowls and the powerful gong. bhaktee.com.

SW. PRAKASHANANDA SARASWATI is a Co-Dharma Heir of Sacred Feet Yoga and lineage holder of the great Indian Saint Bhagavan Nityananda. She is a well-loved Shaktipat Teacher living in the UK. jefifoundation.org/sacred-feet-yoga.

YAELLE SCHWARCZ is a creative heart, writer, soul art guide, and artist who combines her training and experience to invite others to the rhythm of their own beat.

BURGE SMITH-LYONS is founder of Essence of Being, Inc. and The Conscious Leadership Academy. Since 1981 Burge has taught live and online transformational playshops for thousands of men, women, children, and companies on six continents. She is a channel of Shamanaste, certified rebirther, hypnotherapist, intuitive healer, ordained minister, motivational speaker, and international bestselling author. essenceofbeing.com shamanaste.com burgesmithlyons.com.

JEROEN VAN WIEREN had an experience during a coaching session that changed his outlook on life and led to a deep connection with Spirit in a new and creative way.

ANITA WEEKS is an intuitive empath who helps others to find and live in their power. neetvalues.com.

SARYON MICHAEL WHITE is an author, public speaker, and channel. His first book, *Roya Sands and the Bridge Between Worlds*, is a highly relevant spiritual adventure set in the modern world. saryon.com.

SEANA ZELAZO is an intuitive channel offering spiritual guidance, coaching, and teaching. A licensed clinical social worker, her background includes hospice, private practice psychotherapy and training in many healing modalities. seanazelazo.com.

MEET OUR FEATURED AUTHOR

MARILYN ALAURIA is a gifted psychic medium, teacher, and coach with an unmatched capacity to ignite deep, soul-level transformation for her clients around the world. Marilyn provides messages from guides that are always with us and from loved ones who have crossed over. As the creator of Soul Finder Academy and Membership for Your Soul and host of the podcast Who Can It Be Now, she offers a clear action plan for developing our talents, following our purpose, fulfilling our dreams, and living in alignment with our souls.

After a successful Emmy Award-winning career in the entertainment industry with MTV and NBC Olympics, Marilyn shifted her focus to sharing her natural gifts and helping others discover their own intuitive abilities and living a life from the seat of their soul. She teaches spirituality in a way that leads to a practical, meaningful, and joyous life—no unicorns, flying carpets, or impossible routines required. Marilyn simplifies the path to living a life of peace, ease, and alignment, making true fulfillment easy and achievable. As a psychic medium, healer, teacher, author, and speaker, she lights up audiences around the world and is devoted to using her abilities to bring awareness and enlightenment to every life she touches.

Learn more at marilynalauria.com.

Made in the USA
Las Vegas, NV
20 June 2022